EXTREME
NATURAL
DISASTERS

Produced for HarperCollins by:

HYDRA PUBLISHING
129 MAIN STREET
IRVINGTON, NY 10533
WWW.HYLASPUBLISHING.COM

FIRST EDITION

The name of the "Smithsonian," "Smithsonian Institution," and the sunburst logo are registered trademarks of the Smithsonian Institution.

Library of Congress Cataloging-in-Publication Data
Gibson, Christine.
  Extreme natural disasters / Christine Gibson.
    p. cm.
  Includes index.
  ISBN 978-0-06-089143-5
  1. Natural disasters. I. Title.

GB5014.G53 2007
363.34--dc22

07 08 09 10   QW   10 9 8 7 6 5 4 3 2 1

EXTREME
NATURAL
DISASTERS

Collins

An Imprint of HarperCollinsPublishers

Christine Gibson

Contents

Below: Boat flipped upside down onto a Louisiana dock during the 2005 hurricane season.

Opposite page: Hurricane Carol created giant waves, which smashed beachfront houses on Connecticut's coast in 1954.

Earth's Destructive Power

When the United States dropped the bomb called Little Boy at Hiroshima, Japan, in August 1945, the world got its first glimpse of the overwhelming impact of nuclear weapons. Today, that unnatural event remains the benchmark for the power and destruction of natural disasters. These events are often said to have devastated an area X times as large as Hiroshima, or to have carried the force of a certain number of atomic bombs. These figures are almost always many times greater than the benchmark to which they are being compared. Human-built arsenals cannot begin to match the destructive power of the forces of nature. With towering walls of water and incandescent currents of glowing lava, the Earth asserts its dominance, again and again.

Unstable Planet

Disaster can attack from above or below, from the clouds or the ground. Weather disasters, such as storms, floods, and drought, remind us of the precarious balance between the elements that support life on Earth. An increase or decrease in any of the atmosphere's characteristics—too hot, too cold, too wet, or too dry—can be catastrophic. Earthquakes and volcanoes, on the other hand, hint at the churning cauldron beneath our feet.

Despite Earth's seemingly static surface, the continents collide and the inner layers of the globe boil. When a land-mass jumps or molten lava bursts free, populations see their homes crumble and their loved ones die.

Human Influence

We do not live on a placid planet: The wind blows, the water rises, and the ground moves. As populations grow and spread, they must often wrestle with the environment in order to settle. Unfortunately, human interference often generates a reaction. Stripping a dry region for farmland results in a dust bowl; burning too much petroleum changes the atmosphere. Even attempts to prevent calamity can backfire. The U.S. Army Corps of Engineers tried to cage the lower Mississippi

Opposite page: The eruption of Mount Colo in Kololio, Indonesia, spared Una Una island, pictured here.

Below: A K9 search-and-rescue handler and her dog search homes for missing people after Hurricane Katrina.

River, for example, but their levees only intensified its current when the river flooded in 1927.

There are ways in which humans can defend themselves against nature's fury. Maintaining the natural ecosystem helps to mitigate floods and drought, and well-placed trees can block avalanches. And while storm clouds and volcanoes cannot be defused, or earthquakes calmed, their devastating effects on people and property can be lessened through preparedness. Scientists have made great strides in predicting all kinds of disasters, and societies, chastened by recurring tragedy, have begun to fortify against the inevitable.

What Makes a Disaster?

A hurricane or an earthquake in a remote area is not considered a natural disaster. From Tokyo to New Orleans the media has provided chilling images that show the potential for destruction when a cataclysm strikes cities and villages: The extent of the carnage depends on both the force of the event and its location. If aimed directly at a population center, even a small event can prove lethal. A 50-mile dogleg in the path of a hurricane or tornado can mean the difference between nuisance and tragedy. Unfortunately, humans tend to hug the world's coasts, where the sea and sky conspire to brew monster squalls.

In an even crueler twist, disaster tends to punish those least capable of putting up a fight. Quakes in Kashmir, droughts in Africa, flood after flood in Bangladesh: Over and over, the Earth pummels people who are already starving and homeless and who possess only meager resources with which to recover or rebuild. Disasters never occur in a vacuum. They demolish towns, rend families, and bankrupt governments. Victims suffer lingering effects—social, political, economic, and cultural—long after the skies clear and the ground stills.

So why do people continue to live in these volatile regions? In some places, such as the Nile River valley, a catastrophe can deliver benefits, as floods can deposit fertile soil. In other cases, denial reigns. People instinctively expect the world to continue to behave as it has during their lifetime. If a volcano has not erupted for many years, it might stay asleep; if the rain is falling now, it probably always will; if a fault in the Earth's crust has remained inactive

Below: Collapsed buildings in Mexico City after the 1985 earthquake.

Background: Flooded areas of New Orleans after Hurricane Katrina, in 2005.

Opposite page, top: Wreckage of a Georgia business hit by tornadoes in March 2007.

Opposite page, bottom: An elevated highway that collapsed in the 1994 earthquake that caused major damage in Northridge, California.

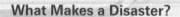

for a century, perhaps the prophesied earthquake will never come. Even when disaster is imminent, residents may see the signs but refuse to flee. Variations on that story weave throughout these pages, always with tragic endings.

Extreme Natural Disasters provides gripping accounts of these terrible events, along with stories of nick-of-time escapes, heroic rescues, and triumphant discoveries. Sometimes the Earth plays the villain and sometimes the reacting victim, but its gestures are invariably awe-inspiring. The present generation should pay attention: These tales are our past, and also our future.

Where in the World?

Continental United States and Canada

1 Eastern U.S.: Blizzard, 1993
2 Eastern U.S.: Hurricane Floyd, 1999
3 Eastern Canada and Eastern U.S.: Ice storm, 1998
4 Boston, MA: Earthquake, 1755
5 Johnstown, PA: Flood, 1889
6 La Plata, MD: Tornado, 2002
7 South Florida: Hurricane Wilma, 2005
8 Louisiana: Hurricane Katrina, 2005
9 Moore, OK: Tornadoes, 1998, 1999, 2003
10 Mississippi River: Flood, 1927
11 New Madrid, MO: Earthquakes, 1811–12
12 Southern Great Plains: Dust Bowl, 1930s
13 Alaska through California: Tsunami, 1946
14 San Francisco, CA: Earthquake, 1906
15 California: Wildfires and drought, 2003
16 Wellington, WA: Avalanche, 1910
17 Washington: Mount St. Helens volcano, 1980

Hawaii

18 Hilo: Tsunami, 1946
19 Big island: Kilauea volcano, ongoing eruptions
20 All islands: Tsunami, 1960

Mexico

21 Mexico City: Earthquake, 1985
22 Yucatán Peninsula: Hurricane Wilma, 2005
23 Gulf Coast: Hurricane Stan, 2005

Central America and Caribbean

23 Central America: Hurricane Stan, 2005
24 Guatemala: Mudslides, 2005
25 Montserrat: Soufrière Hills volcano, 1995
26 Martinique: Mount Pelée volcano, 1902
27 Cuba: Hurricane Wilma, 2005
28 Honduras and Nicaragua: Hurricane Mitch, 1998

South America

29 Colombia: Nevado del Ruiz volcano, 1985
30 Peru and Ecuador: Drought (ongoing)
31 Peru and Ecuador: Floods, 1982–83
32 Peru: Avalanche, 1970
33 Chile: Earthquake and tsunami, 1960
34 West coast: Flood, 1997–98

Europe

35 Munich, Germany: Hailstorm, 1984
36 Italy: Mount Vesuvius volcano, 79 CE and 1639
37 Entire continent: Heat wave, 2003
38 Entire continent: Year of No Summer, 1816
39 Central Europe: Floods, 1997–98

Iceland

40 Entire country: Ongoing volcanic eruptions

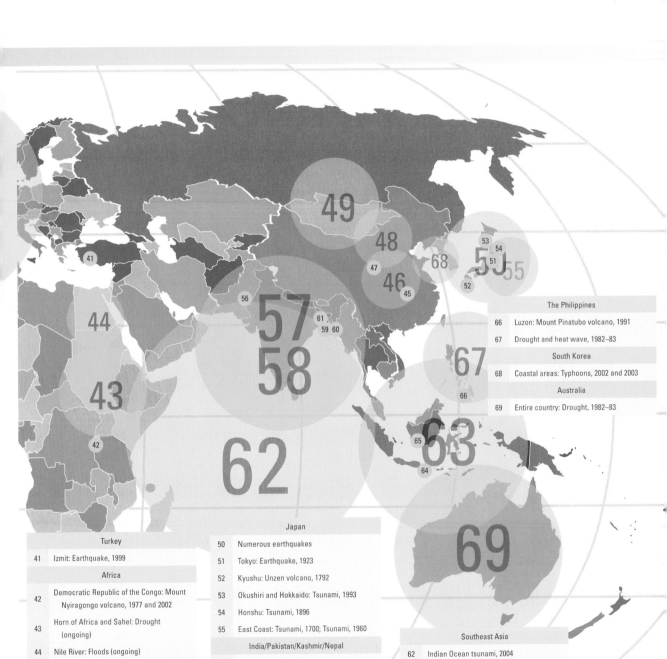

The Philippines

66	Luzon: Mount Pinatubo volcano, 1991
67	Drought and heat wave, 1982–83

South Korea

68	Coastal areas: Typhoons, 2002 and 2003

Australia

69	Entire country: Drought, 1982–83

Turkey

41	Izmit: Earthquake, 1999

Africa

42	Democratic Republic of the Congo: Mount Nyiragongo volcano, 1977 and 2002
43	Horn of Africa and Sahel: Drought (ongoing)
44	Nile River: Floods (ongoing)

China/Mongolia

45	Henan Province: Hailstorm, 2002
46	Yangtze River: Flood, 1931–32
47	Shaanxi: Earthquake, 1556
48	Inner Mongolia and northern China: Drought (ongoing)
49	Mongolia: Heat wave, 1997–98

Japan

50	Numerous earthquakes
51	Tokyo: Earthquake, 1923
52	Kyushu: Unzen volcano, 1792
53	Okushiri and Hokkaido: Tsunami, 1993
54	Honshu: Tsunami, 1896
55	East Coast: Tsunami, 1700; Tsunami, 1960

India/Pakistan/Kashmir/Nepal

56	Pakistan: Earthquake, 2005
57	India: Heat wave, 2003
58	India: Drought, 1982–83

Bangladesh

59	Ganges Delta: Floods, 1998 and 1999
60	Manikgaj: Tornado, 1989
61	Bhola: Hurricane, 1970

Southeast Asia

62	Indian Ocean tsunami, 2004

Pacific Islands

63	Entire region: Drought, 1982–83 and 1997–98

Indonesia

64	Sumbawa: Tambora volcano, 1815
65	Borneo: Drought and fires, 1982–83 and 1997–98

Prediction, Preparation, and Prevention

Hurricanes

PREDICTION: Although scientists do not yet completely understand the complex conditions within the atmosphere, by keeping close tabs on developing tropical storms and using computer models, they have made remarkable strides in forecasting hurricanes in recent years.

PREPARATION: Homes can be protected from wind damage by reinforcing the roof, shutters, and doors. A disaster supply kit with food and water, first-aid supplies, a charged cell phone, and battery- or hand-crank-operated radio (plus batteries) should be kept on hand. Cars should have a full tank of gas.

PREVENTION: For a couple of decades, the U.S. government experimented with cloud seeding in hurricane rain bands, hoping to encourage thunderstorms that would draw energy from the hurricane. The experiments were not successful. Scientists have since focused on understanding and forecasting hurricanes rather than trying to prevent them.

Tornadoes

PREDICTION: Tornadoes can develop from a range of weather patterns. Forecasters stay on the lookout for atmospheric conditions that have a high degree of moisture, instability, lift, and wind shear.

PREPARATION: People living in tornado-prone areas should determine the safest spot in their homes, offices, and anywhere else they frequent (stores, schools, and so on). Tornado drills should be staged at least once a year.

PREVENTION: Schemes have been suggested to defuse tornados, such as barraging them with dry ice or even bombing them with nuclear weapons, but such schemes are generally impractical or more damaging than the storm would be. For now, tornados are not preventable.

Snowstorms and Ice Storms

PREDICTION: Meteorologists monitor approaching fronts and the moisture in the air.

PREPARATION: Warm clothes, a shovel, and tire chains should be stored in passenger cars, and gas tanks filled up if a blizzard is expected. Flashlights and a battery- or hand-crank-operated radio (plus batteries) should be available at home, as well as enough food and toiletries to last a couple of days.

PREVENTION: Prevention is not possible yet, and human-induced climate change may be increasing snow and ice storms in some places.

Avalanches

PREDICTION: Rangers and forecasters can guess where avalanches are likely to develop by observing the snowpack and identifying treeless slopes and overhangs.

PREPARATION: Skiers and winter mountaineers should travel in groups and carry transceivers and shovels. They should also familiarize themselves with conditions that make avalanches likely.

PREVENTION: Planting thickets of trees in likely avalanche zones may block the snow from sliding. Some engineers also fence dangerous areas with 12-foot-high metal barriers. Rangers may blast large masses of snow with gunfire to break them up. Patrol teams close off unstable slopes.

Above: A tornado-warning siren. Center top: Canned goods, matches, a battery-operated radio, and other items make up a hurricane supply kit. Center bottom: Sandbags are a simple but effective way to reduce floodwater damage. Opposite page: A tsunami evacuation sign.

Floods

PREDICTION: Scientists can determine in advance, through statistical studies and computer models, where floodwater is likely to flow. Most floods are caused by high rainfall or sudden thaws, which are easily monitored.

PREPARATION: Homes should be built on high ground, if possible, using water-resistant materials. A three-day supply of water and nonperishable foods should be kept at hand.

PREVENTION: Levees, embankments, and sandbags can hold back rising waters. Trees and other plants help the ground absorb some excess water, and intact wetlands can hold large quantities of water.

Drought

PREDICTION: Since droughts depend on so many variables, both meteorological and ecological, scientists can at best predict drought about a month in advance. Soil moisture, topography, and air-sea interplay all determine a dry spell's duration.

PREPARATION: Governments in drought-prone areas should stockpile food, water purification systems, and medical supplies; unfortunately, impoverished countries may be unable to prepare for droughts.

PREVENTION: Trees anchor the soil and transpire moisture into the air, encouraging rain. Planting more trees in drought-prone areas may prevent dry spells, and maintaining healthy forests can keep an area from becoming drought-prone.

Earthquakes

PREDICTION: Scientists can predict where, but not exactly when, an earthquake will strike. Analysis of the positions of tectonic plates and their past behavior can help indicate big tremors to come.

PREPARATION: Buildings should be well-braced and anchored to the ground or on special rollers. Residents should identify the safest spots in their homes and offices and practice ducking and covering.

PREVENTION: Prevention is not possible, although researchers have considered trying to control the size of an earthquake by lubricating faults.

Volcanoes

PREDICTION: Earthquakes and sulfurous emissions often precede an eruption. Volcanologists can detect rising magma by measuring tremors and the tilt of the mountain, and they can map likely lava and lahar flow paths. But they cannot pinpoint exactly when a volcano will erupt.

PREPARATION: Establish quick, reliable public-alert networks and evacuation routes.

PREVENTION: Not possible.

Tsunamis

PREDICTION: Tsunamis may be caused by earthquakes, landslides, or volcanic eruptions. When any of these events occur, oceanographers monitor sea levels to determine if a tsunami has been generated.

PREPARATION: Reliable public-alert systems and clearly marked evacuation routes help people escape in advance of the waves.

PREVENTION: Prevention is not possible, although coastal communities can block moderately high waves with seawalls.

The Worst of the Worst

WORST HURRICANES

The ten most intense hurricanes (based on central pressure in millibars) in the Atlantic basin for 1851–2005.

HURRICANE NAME	YEAR	MINIMUM PRESSURE
Wilma	2005	882 mb
Gilbert	1988	888 mb
Unnamed (Labor Day)	1935	892 mb
Rita	2005	895 mb
Allen	1980	899 mb
Katrina	2005	902 mb
Camille	1969	905 mb
Mitch	1998	905 mb
Ivan	2004	910 mb

Deadliest Hurricane, Cyclone, or Typhoon
East Pakistan (now Bangladesh) November 13, 1970, at least 30,000 deaths

TEN LARGEST EARTHQUAKES IN THE WORLD SINCE 1900 (WHEN MEASUREMENT BEGAN)

	LOCATION	DATE	MAGNITUDE
1	Chile	May 22, 1960	9.5
2	Off the west coast of northern Sumatra	December 26, 2004	9.3
3	Prince William Sound, Alaska	March 28, 1964	9.2
4	Kamchatka	November 4, 1952	9.0
5	Off the coast of Ecuador	January 31, 1906	8.8
6	Rat Islands, Alaska	February 3, 1965	8.7
7	Northern Sumatra, Indonesia	March 28, 2005	8.6
8	Andreanof Islands, Alaska	March 9, 1957	8.6
9	Assam–Tibet	August 15, 1950	8.6
10	Kuril Islands	October 13, 1963	8.5

TEN DEADLIEST U.S. TORNADOES

	STATE(S)	DATE	TIME	DEATHS	INJURED	F-SCALE	AFFECTED TOWNS
1	MO-IL-IN	March 18, 1925	1:01 PM	695	2,027	F-5	Murphysboro, Gorham, DeSoto
2	LA-MS	May 7, 1840	1:45 PM	317	109	?	Natchez
3	MO-IL	May 27, 1896	6:30 PM	255	1,000	F-4	St. Louis, East St. Louis
4	MS	April 5, 1936	8:55 PM	216	700	F-5	Tupelo
5	GA	April 6, 1936	8:27 AM	203	1,600	F-4	Gainesville
6	TX-OK-KS	April 9, 1947	6:05 PM	181	970	F-5	Glazier, Higgins, Woodward
7	LA-MS	April 24, 1908	11:45 AM	143	770	F-4	Amite, Pine, Purvis
8	WI	June 12, 1899	5:40 PM	117	200	F-5	New Richmond
9	MI	June 8, 1953	8:30 PM	115	844	F-5	Flint
10	TX	May 11, 1953	4:10 PM	114	597	F-5	Waco

World's Deadliest Tornado

Bangladesh, April 26, 1989
1,300 deaths

TEN COSTLIEST U.S. TORNADOES (IN 2003 DOLLARS)

	DATE	LOCATION(S)	COST
1	March 31, 1973	Central-northern GA	5,175,000,000
2	June 8, 1966	Topeka, KS	1,420,000,000
3	May 11, 1970	Lubbock, TX	1,185,000,000
4	May 3, 1999	Oklahoma City, OK	1,100,000,000
5	April 3, 1974	Xenia, OH	932,500,000
6	May 6, 1975	Omaha, NE	857,062,260
7	April 10, 1979	Wichita Falls, TX	702,937,730
8	June 3, 1980	Grand Island, NE	635,661,500
9	October 3, 1979	Windsor Locks, CT	632,500,000
10	May 8, 2003	Oklahoma City, OK	370,000,000

TEN DEADLIEST EARTHQUAKES

	LOCATION	DATE	DEATHS	MAGNITUDE, IF MEASURED
1	Shaanxi, China	January 23, 1556	830,000	
2	Sumatra, Indonesia	December 26, 2004	28,3106 (includes tsunami deaths)	9.1
3	Tangshan, China	July 27, 1976	255,000 (official; estimated death toll as high as 655,000)	7.5
4	Aleppo, Syria	August 9, 1138	230,000	
5	Damghan, Iran	December 22, 856	200,000	
6	Tsinghai, China	May 22, 1927	200,000	7.9
7	Gansu, China	December 16, 1920	200,000	7.8
8	Ardabil, Iran	March 23, 893	150,000	
9	Kanto (Kwanto), Japan	September 1, 1923	143,000 (caused Great Tokyo Fire)	7.9
10	Turkmenistan, Ashgabat	October 5, 1948	110,000	7.3

TEN DEADLIEST ERUPTIONS

	DEATHS	VOLCANO	YEAR	MAJOR CAUSE OF DEATH
1	92,000	Tambora, Indonesia	1815	Starvation
2	36,417	Krakatau, Indonesia	1883	Tsunami
3	29,025	Pelée, Martinique	1902	Ash flows
4	25,000	Ruiz, Colombia	1985	Mudflows
5	14,300	Unzen, Japan	1792	Volcano collapse, tsunami
6	9,350	Laki, Iceland	1783	Starvation
7	5,110	Kelut, Indonesia	1919	Mudflows
8	4,011	Galunggung, Indonesia	1882	Mudflows
9	3,500	Vesuvius, Italy	1631	Mudflows, lava flows
10	3,360	Vesuvius, Italy	79	Ash flows and falls

TEN DEADLIEST TSUNAMIS			
	DEATHS	YEAR	MAGNITUDE	LOCATION
1	225,000+	2004	9.3	Indian Ocean
2	100,000	1645 (?) BCE		Crete-Santorini, Ancient Greece
3	60,000	1755	8.5	Portugal, Morocco
4	40,000	1782	7.0	South China Sea
5	36,500	1883		Krakatau, Indonesia
6	30,000	1707		Tokaido-Nankaido, Japan
7	26,360	1896	7.6	Sanriku, Japan
8	25,674	1868	8.5	Northern Chile
9	15,030	1792	6.4	Kyushu Island, Japan
10	13,486	1771	7.4	Ryukyu Trench, Japan

Deadliest Drought
China, 1876-79, 9 million deaths

Worst Volcanoes
· Most voluminous eruption: Tambora
· Highest death toll: Tambora
· Loudest: Krakatau
· Deadliest pyroclastic flow: Pelée

Largest Recorded Earthquake in the United States
Prince William Sound, Alaska, March 28, 1964, magnitude 9.2

Most Disastrous Snowstorms and Ice Storms
· Most damage from a snowstorm: March 1993, eastern United States
· Greatest snowfall: 1971–72, Paradise, Mount Rainier, 1,122 inches (28.5 m)
· Deepest snow: Tamarac, CA, March 1911, 37.5 feet (11.43 m)
· Costliest blizzard in U.S. history: 1993—$2 billion–$6 billion
· Heaviest recorded hail: Bangladesh on April 14, 1986, stones weighing as much as 2.2 pounds (1 kg)
· Largest single hailstone: Aurora, NE, 2003, with a circumference of 18.75 inches (48 cm)

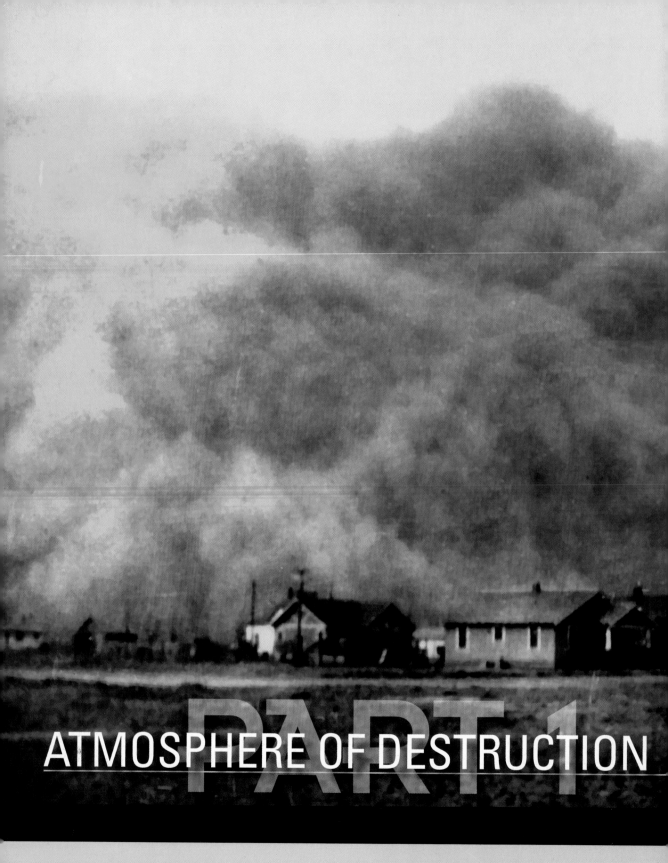

ATMOSPHERE OF DESTRUCTION

PART 1

CHAPTER 1

HURRICANES

HURRICANES, CYCLONES, TYPHOONS. These are all different names for the same type of storm—the biggest storms on Earth.

Even though tornadoes may clock higher winds, hurricanes are usually much deadlier, both because of their size—hurricane systems can reach 500 miles (805 km) across—and because of the amount of water they move.

Hurricanes cause devastation all over the world, but they are all born in the same latitudes—the tropics. This is where the main ingredients of a hurricane reside: warm oceans at 80° Fahrenheit (26.5°C) or more, warm air, light wind, and moisture in the atmosphere. Yet while all these ingredients exist for much of the summer in tropical climates, they do not always result in deadly storms. The catalyst needed for these conditions to become a hurricane is an atmospheric disturbance.

A tropical disturbance, or cluster of thunderstorms, might occur when a cold front skips down into the tropics and runs up against the walls of warm air. Or it may start with a low-pressure system spinning around the atmosphere and landing down near the water. Either way, when the conditions are right, the storm will start to get organized and spin into a tropical depression with a low-pressure system at the center.

Left: A satellite photo of Hurricane Epsilon from December 4, 2005, four days after the end of the official Atlantic hurricane season. Epsilon was the fifth hurricane to form outside the season in 150 years; it was also the longest-lived December hurricane ever recorded, a fitting end to a record-breaking season. Inset: Eight days after the deadliest hurricane in history hit East Pakistan (now Bangladesh) in November 1970, children in Bhola received meals from the first relief supplies to reach the area. Pages 12–13: A wall of dust approaches Stratford, Texas. Severe drought combined with poor soil-conservation methods turned the U.S. Great Plains into what became known as the Dust Bowl.

From Disturbance to Storm

A hurricane is formed when warm, damp air is drawn into a storm forming just above the surface of the ocean (top illustration). The air rises and cools, causing its moisture to condense and release heat. The surrounding air absorbs the heat and expands outward from the center of the storm, lowering the pressure at the surface. The lower pressure draws more moist air into the system, which intensifies in a continuous loop until land, cooler water, or high wind shear slow it down. As the storm intensifies (bottom illustration), moist air is drawn upward before it even reaches the center. In between thunderstorm regions are dry pockets of cool, sinking air.

A tropical depression has winds circulating up to 38 miles per hour (61 km/h). As this potential hurricane sits over the warm tropical waters, the low-pressure zone in its center acts as a vacuum, pulling clouds toward it.

At the same time, the ocean is adding energy to the storm. Warm water changes into water vapor and rises off the ocean's surface. As the water vapor cools, it releases heat energy into the air. The heated air moves faster, pulling in more air and water around it. When winds reach between 39 and 73 miles per hour (63 and 117 km/h), the tropical depression becomes a tropical storm.

The water vapor that has cooled becomes water droplets. These collect into even bigger thunderclouds, and the storm grows. As the storm gets taller, it hits the stratosphere and flattens out at the top. As long as there is a supply of warm water, the system continues to grow stronger winds and bigger clouds. Once winds reach 74 miles per hour (119 km/h) or more, the storm is classified as a hurricane.

With so much wind, the storm system has to move. Most hurricanes just move around in the ocean until the water cools and the storm falls apart. Some may begin to disintegrate and then pick up speed again, as a new source of warm water appears. The storm will eventually die, once it either hits cold water or stays on dry land long enough. Without warm water as an energy source, the hurricane will dissipate.

These potent storms that go by many names are among the most destructive forces known, and the combination of this tempestuous force with civilization can lead to disaster.

Hurricane Hunting

Hurricane prediction and monitoring is a team sport. "Hurricane hunters" fly inside the storm to measure air pressure while satellites take measurements from the outside.

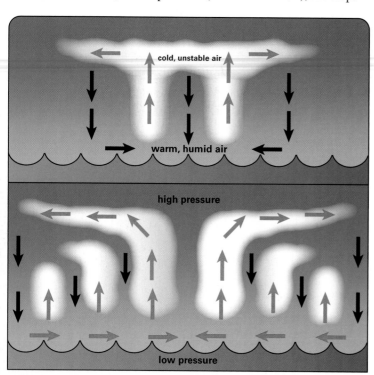

Hurricanes can only form over areas where the ocean surface is about 80°F (26.5°C). This map, compiled using satellite data from June 2002 to September 2003, shows those regions in orange; zones where the water surface was below 82°F are shown in blue.

In the United States, personnel from the Air Force Reserves and the National Oceanic and Atmospheric Administration (NOAA) fly into the storm to take on-the-spot measurements. Knowing the internal pressure is key to knowing if the storm is building or dying out. The planes fly in low, at altitudes between 500 and 1,500 feet (152 and 457 m) and make the return trip at higher altitudes. Among other tasks, the hurricane hunters release a dropsonde, a weather-sensing canister, that radios back information about humidity, temperature, air pressure, and wind speed as it falls to the water's surface. The plane's crew sends the information to a satellite, which relays it to the National Weather Service.

What Do Satellites Measure?

WIND SPEEDS. Satellites measure rotating surface winds when a storm is still in its infancy.

SEA TEMPERATURES. Using microwave imaging, satellites can detect sea-surface temperatures. This information helps forecasters predict if storms are likely to gain strength or weaken.

AIR TEMPERATURE AND HUMIDITY. Satellites use an infrared system to read the air temperature and humidity at various spots around the world. This information goes into the forecasting system.

TOWER HEIGHT. Inside a tropical depression, massive thunderclouds, called towers, build up. Satellites use infrared wavelengths to detect cloud temperatures and heights. Larger thunderclouds can indicate that a storm will intensify into a hurricane. A satellite called the Tropical Rainfall Measuring Mission (TRMM) uses a microwave-imaging system to scan the interior of storms and measure the towers.

DIRECTION. A series of satellites keep track of storms after they develop. With repeated pictures of a storm's direction and speed, forecasters can better predict where the storm is likely to go.

COMPUTER MODELS. Using all the data from the satellites, airplanes, dropsonde, and ground systems, computer models predict the course and intensity of the storms. Emergency personnel use these predictions to help remove people from harm's way.

One of the National Oceanic and Atmospheric Administration's WP-3D Orion turboprop "hurricane hunter" aircraft flies above the eye (the blue spot just below the plane) of a hurricane.

Katrina: Monster Storm

Floodwaters from Hurricane Katrina threaten to submerge a highway overpass in 2005. Heavy rain, 20-foot (6 m) storm surges, and failing levees flooded more than 70 percent of New Orleans at the end of August. Hundreds of people died, and tens of thousands were stranded without food, potable water, or shelter.

New Orleans, Louisiana, sits near the mouth of the Mississippi River on some of the most fertile land on Earth. This low-lying city, which is virtually surrounded by the Gulf of Mexico, the Mississippi River, and Lake Pontchartrain, was not built to withstand a large hurricane. Eighty percent of the city is below sea level. So when meteorologists saw Hurricane Katrina headed straight for the city, they braced themselves for the worst. And then the worst came, but not in the ways the meteorologists had expected.

Katrina formed over the Bahamas on August 23, 2005. After sending a few winds across Florida, the storm moved into the Gulf of Mexico, where it grew to become one of the most powerful storms ever recorded. By the time Katrina blew toward Louisiana, the storm was as big as the state of Maryland.

City Plans

New Orleans officials had considered what would happen in the event of a big hurricane, but a viable plan was

Hurricane Katrina moves over southern Mississippi at 9:02 AM on August 29, 2005, after inundating New Orleans earlier that morning. Although it had already begun to weaken by the time of this satellite photo, the storm was still barraging the Gulf Coast with 135 mile per hour (217 km/h) winds, storm surges, and torrential rains. Katrina was one of the strongest hurricanes ever to strike the United States.

not in place as the storm approached. On August 27, President George W. Bush declared a state of emergency in Louisiana, Alabama, and Mississippi.

On August 28, when Katrina was upgraded to a category 5 storm, Mayor Ray Nagin ordered a mandatory evacuation. Now it was the law: People had to leave. It has been estimated that 80 percent of the 1.3 million residents did evacuate. But the mayor's order had no effect for people who did not have the means to get out.

Roads were jammed. Airlines were overbooked. As the storm progressed, escape routes became flooded. Buses and taxis that might have been used to move more people to higher ground were underwater.

City officials had established "refuges of last resort," emergency shelters that included the Louisiana Superdome stadium and convention center, for what they predicted would be about 26,000 people who would not be able to get out of the city. But with escape

On the Love Avenue Canal in New Orleans in March 2006, workers from the U.S. Army Corps of Engineers prepare structural beams to support new levee gates. The original levees were not designed with adequate strength, causing them to fail after Hurricane Katrina.

looking less and less possible, the city still had hundreds of thousands of residents and tourists waiting out the winds and water.

No Defense

On August 29, at 6 AM, Katrina made landfall at Buras-Triumph, Louisiana, about 60 miles (96 km) southeast of the heart of the Crescent City. New Orleans and towns and cities within a 120-mile (193 km) radius felt the impact. Katrina had weakened to a category 3 hurricane, but it was still huge.

Hurricanes are not new to the Gulf Coast, but they become costlier every year as more and more buildings go up

along the shore and natural barriers are destroyed. In the past, extensive coastal wetlands acted like sponges, helping to keep floodwaters in check. Now, thousands of acres of wetlands have been converted to cities and agricultural fields, and levees built to keep the Mississippi River from overflowing its banks also cause the wetlands to disappear. The cypress trees, which had once surrounded the coast and acted as a windbreak, are nearly gone. This lack of natural defense, coupled with the growth of cities—in both population and urban development—has led to increased damage and greater cost in the event of a hurricane.

When Katrina hit land, there was nothing to hold it back. Houses on the Gulf Coast were carried away or destroyed. Whole communities disappeared into the waves. The hurricane bounced back and then struck land a second time at 10 AM. In New Orleans, the winds had cut off electricity. Water from the storm surge took over the roads and drove through the streets to the lowest parts of the city, completely flooding the section called the lower ninth ward. As Katrina moved out of the area, the people of New Orleans breathed more easily.

The Real Flood

Everyone knew that the storm surge would be bad and flooding would result. But then they thought the water would recede, damage reports would be posted, and life would go back to normal. The trouble was that the water did not recede.

The storm surge started greater floods by sending waves up the canals into Lake Pontchartrain. The levees that were built to hold the lake back from the Mississippi basin failed, causing a seemingly endless supply of water to pour in.

Water stops at nothing. It climbs steps and goes under doors, leaving ruin in its wake. Residents climbed onto their roofs to avoid the water. Grabbing anything that would float and anything they could row with, some people managed to paddle to safety. Some paddled back to help those who could not help themselves—the children, the elderly, and the ill.

Two weeks after Katrina, much of New Orleans was still flooded. In addition to rainwater and storm surges, water from nearby Lake Pontchartrain bled into the city, most of which is below sea level. Engineers had to repair the electrical grid and most of the city's 148 pumps before the streets were finally cleared of floodwater.

Water pours through a break in the levee along Industrial Canal in New Orleans on August 31, 2005. This was one of many of the city's canal levees that disintegrated under Katrina's waves and storm surges. In the top half of the photograph, neighborhoods lie underwater from breaches in other canal walls.

More than 70 percent of New Orleans flooded. Hundreds of people died. Rescue helicopters picked up people from their roofs and from highway overpasses. But there was not enough help, and those who were rescued still had more problems to face.

The city no longer had a center. Food was scarce. Some people stole food and necessities, while others stole luxury goods simply because they could. Television images showed looters, National Guard soldiers, and fleeing residents all wading through the streets chest-deep in the water.

Rescued and evacuated people made their way to the Superdome. The refuges of last resort suddenly held hundreds of thousands of hungry, frightened citizens. Supplies were insufficient and hygiene facilities were overflowing. Many later described it as hell.

Engineers frantically worked to get the levees patched and the city's pump

What would be saved and what would be sacrificed? These daunting choices had to be made by individual survivors and local and national government officials. How much aid should individuals get, and for how long? And who was responsible for the failed levees and the failed evacuation?

As towns continue to rebuild, these questions still haunt those who lived in Katrina's path, as well as the nation that witnessed the devastation.

system online. When the water finally started to recede, buses arrived to evacuate people to Dallas or Houston. Some people went to Arkansas, others as far as Detroit. Cities and towns all over the country began taking in refugees. Huge refugee centers were set up with cots, food, towels, and other necessities but little privacy. After more time, displaced residents were given vouchers to pay for apartments and hotels.

In the meantime, New Orleans created Web sites to connect the refugees with their families. They set up morgues and tried to identify the bodies of more than 1,600 people who had died in the storm or in the subsequent flooding.

Katrina caused over $80 billion in damages, earning the title of the most costly Atlantic hurricane. And the dollar amount does not take into account the emotional cost of the ongoing cleanup.

HURRICANE LEVELS: SAFFIR-SIMPSON HURRICANE SCALE

The Saffir-Simpson scale was developed in 1969 by civil engineer Herbert Saffir and Bob Simpson, who was the director of the U.S. National Hurricane Center at the time. It is used to give an estimate of the potential property damage and flooding expected along the coast. The categories are based primarily on wind speed.

Category	Description
1	Winds 74 to 95 miles per hour (119–153 km/h)
2	Winds 96 to 110 mph (154–177 km/h)
3	Winds 111 to 130 mph (178–209 km/h)
4	Winds 131 to 155 mph (179–249 km/h)
5	Winds greater than 155 mph (>250 km/h)

Hurricane Wilma: The World's Most Intense Storm

Hurricane Wilma broke records even before it threatened the land. On October 19, 2005, Wilma whipped up from a tropical storm to the most intense category 5 hurricane ever recorded. The intensity of a hurricane is found by measuring the pressure at the center of the storm in units called millibars (mb). The lower the pressure, the more intense the hurricane.

Much of a hurricane's strength is seen in its wind speed, but its driving force is the central pressure. The central pressure is the difference between the hurricane's pressure and the pressure in the air around it. And central pressure is what feeds the hurricane new winds. Until Wilma appeared, Hurricane Mitch (1998) had held the record-breaking lowest pressure, measured at 905 millibars. Then Wilma came in at the super-low level

SPECIFICATIONS

HURRICANE WILMA, 2005
Formed: October 15, 2005
Dissipated: October 25, 2005
Highest wind speed: 185 mph (295 km/h)
Wind speed at landfall: 125 mph (201 km/h)
Lowest pressure: 882 mb
Damage: over $25 billion (2005 US$)
Deaths: 23 direct, 40 indirect

of 882 millibars. Researchers knew the hurricane was gaining power, sucking new wind into the low-pressure center.

Yucatán — Cuba — Key West

On October 21, Wilma hit Mexico's Yucatán Peninsula with winds of 125 miles per hour (201 km/h). Sitting on Cancún for 32 hours, Wilma damaged about 80 percent of the hotels in the tourist area and pulled apart the airport. While only eight people were killed, looting was a major problem, and the emergency shelters were not prepared for the influx of people. Mexico's president Vicente Fox told the *Economist* that rebuilding would cost on the order of $2.7 billion and that the economic impact would be felt for years to come.

Gaining strength from the warm ocean, Wilma sent a waist-deep storm surge into Havana, Cuba. The Cuban government reported $704 million in damages, affecting the fishing, wood,

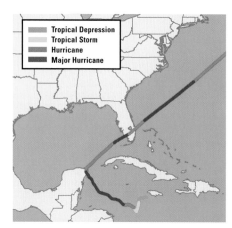

The life span of a powerful storm. Between its birth as a low-pressure system in the Caribbean in the second week of October 2005 and its absorption by another low southeast of Nova Scotia on October 26, Wilma battered the Yucatán peninsula, Cuba, and south Florida. It reached its highest intensity—with the lowest central pressure ever recorded—on October 19, two days before hitting Mexico.

Tropical Depression
Tropical Storm
Hurricane
Major Hurricane

honey, transportation, and construction industries, as well as more than 7,000 damaged homes. And the storm was not yet finished.

Hitting the west coast of Florida, Wilma plowed across the peninsula at a stately pace of 20 to 30 miles per hour (32 to 48 km/h), with winds clocked at 125 miles per hour (201 km/h) taking down trees, buildings, and power lines from Naples to Miami. Ninety percent of the mobile homes in East Naples were destroyed. The strip of destruction damaged water, power, and sewage systems in most of southern Florida. The only available drinking water was supplied by relief agencies.

The storm surge put the Key West islands under 3 to 6 feet (0.9 to 1.8 m) of water. And the major losses in sugar cane and orange crops not only caused economic damage to the state as a whole, but left thousands of migrant workers jobless.

All told, Hurricane Wilma caused 62 deaths and $12 billion in damages.

Ocean surface temperatures from October 15, 2005, the day Wilma formed as a tropical depression, to October 20, when it turned northwest toward landfall on the Yucatán. Yellow, orange, and red represent areas at or above 82°F (27.8°C), the minimum surface temperature required for a hurricane. Temperatures around Wilma held at about 85° (29°C).

RECORD-BREAKING YEAR

The Atlantic hurricane season of 2005 was a record breaker. Of 28 named storms, 15 were hurricanes. The previous record was 21 named storms in 1933, followed by 12 hurricanes in 1969.

Four storms registered at some point as category 5—Emily, Katrina, Wilma, and Rita. The previous record was set in 1960, with two in this category. The single costliest hurricane of all time was Katrina, which was also one of the three strongest hurricanes ever to hit the United States, along with Rita and Wilma.

In 2005, five names were retired because of the cost of these hurricanes, both in terms of dollars and human lives. These hurricanes were Dennis, Emily, Katrina, Rita, and Wilma. Together the storms took 2,280 lives and cost over $100 billion.

Floyd: Far-Flung Destruction

Many hurricanes start in the ocean off Africa, and many die there. But Floyd sucked up energy from the warm waters and grew until, on September 14, 1999, it became one of the farthest-reaching storms North America had ever seen. Spreading destruction from the Bahamas to Newfoundland, Canada, Floyd killed 57 people, caused 13 states to file for disaster relief, and caused approximately 3 million people to leave their homes in one of the largest peacetime evacuations in the history of the United States.

Floyd came in howling. With winds measured at 155 miles per hour (249 km/h) and waves up to 50 feet (15 m) high, Floyd hit the Bahamian islands of San Salvador, Cat, Eleuthera, and Abaco on September 13–14, then went back out to sea for a bit, toying with the people on the coast of Florida.

Hurricane Floyd, as captured by NASA's Sea-Viewing Wide Field-of-View Sensor (SeaWiFS), smothers a large section of the eastern United States. The storm spread rain and destruction from the Bahamas to Newfoundland over a week in September 1999, causing $4.5 billion in damage.

State of Emergency

The hurricane warning system was working. Residents knew, governors knew, and President Bill Clinton knew what was going on. Before the hurricane reached the North American coastline, the president called in from New Zealand and declared Florida and Georgia federal disaster areas. The declaration of a state of emergency so early on is common practice with big hurricanes. It speeds the release of relief funds and gives the Federal Emergency Management Agency (FEMA) the authority to coordinate across state lines.

Everyone was as ready as they could be, with houses boarded up and emergency supplies brought in. People evacuated. In the Florida panhandle, Interstate 95 was clogged as people drove north toward Georgia

> "The entire community is underwater,
> literally to the eaves of the buildings."
> —CHRISTINE TODD WHITMAN, GOVERNOR OF NEW JERSEY

Edgecombe County, North Carolina, which is about 120 miles (193 km) inland, lies under muddy water September 19, 1999, three days after Hurricane Floyd first hit the mainland at Cape Terror. Floyd's rains deluged the state's already saturated shore just weeks after Hurricane Dennis passed through.

and Alabama. In North Carolina they moved west, pushing the limits of the little roads at the Outer Banks, aiming for the mountains, or even a church hall with the promise of emergency generators, food, warmth, and security from the storm. Then they waited for the winds.

Floyd taunted them, defying the forecasters who said landfall would be on the eastern shore of Florida.

Relieved, Florida residents kept watching as the storm skipped over the Georgia coast and kept going, even passing up South Carolina. Finally, at North Carolina's Cape Terror, Floyd blew in, less fierce than when it had hit the Bahamas. Winds of 105 miles per hour (169 km/h) made this a category 2 hurricane. But the winds were not the gravest concern. It was the water.

STORM SURGE: DEADLY DOME OF WATER

A storm surge is the dome of abnormally high water created by a hurricane. Three factors lead to this surge: the huge amount of water a hurricane carries in its storm clouds, the winds pushing on surface water, and the low atmospheric pressure associated with hurricanes that can cause higher water levels. Surges are often as much as 50 miles (80 km) across and can be even more damaging if they occur during a particularly high tide. Often centered on the hurricane's eye where atmospheric pressure is lowest, storm surges have been known to reach over 40 feet (12 m) in height.

Computer models are used to predict storm-surge levels. The National Hurricane Center manages a model called the Sea, Lake, Overland Surges for Hurricanes (SLOSH) model. Emergency managers use these models to determine how much of a city's population should be evacuated.

The Deluge

Floyd brought torrential rain to the Carolinas, where the coastline was already soggy from Hurricane Dennis's visit a few weeks before. As Floyd bounced out to sea again and continued north to Long Island in New York, the rains also traveled northward, reaching Newfoundland, Canada, before petering out.

All along the coast, the floods came. Newport News, Virginia, got 17 inches (43 cm) of rain, while 13 inches (33 cm) fell in Somerville, New Jersey, and another 12 inches (30 cm) in Vernon, Delaware. In Bound Brook, New Jersey, the Raritan River flooded, sending 12 feet (3.6 m) of water down Main Street and drowning three people.

But the part of North Carolina near the hurricane's landfall suffered the worst of it. The Tar River leapt from its banks, exceeding 500-year flood marks, burying towns in its way. Downtown Tarboro was underwater for several days. The levees near

SPECIFICATIONS

HURRICANE FLOYD, 1999
Formed: September 7, 1999
Dissipated: September 19, 1999
Highest wind speed: 155 mph (250 km/h)
Lowest pressure: 921 mb
Damage: $5.1 billion (2005 US$)
Deaths: 57 direct, 20 to 30 indirect

By September 21, 1999, when this photograph was taken, the water in downtown Franklin, Virginia, had begun to recede from its maximum height of 6 feet (1.8 m). Leaking gas and propane tanks, chemical barrels, and pesticides made the floodwaters particularly hazardous.

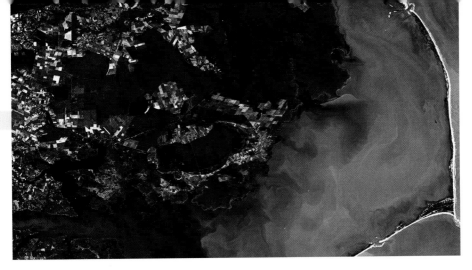

A satellite image shows the sediment flushed into the ocean by Floyd's torrential rains. Silt and waste choked rivers in North Carolina, and scientists feared ocean fish and shrimp would ingest the polluted water. Fortunately, this did not happen. Scientists think it may be because the fish and shellfish prefer saltier water and had moved farther out to sea to escape the freshwater runoff caused by heavy rains in the weeks prior to Floyd.

Princeville failed and the town was submerged under 20 feet (6 m) of water for 10 days.

The Neuse River also jumped its banks, taking houses, farms, and farm animals with it. Thousands of hogs floated alongside mattresses, dressers, and beds. Feces from the farms and waste from sewage systems and industrial sites added to the swirling cauldron, making the river look and smell like something out of Dante's *Inferno*. Floyd's damage totaled about $4.5 billion.

Recovery experts predicted grave environmental damage to the shrimp and fish populations off the North Carolina coast. The polluted water poured out into the ocean and the fish that lived near the river would soon ingest it. Fortunately their dire warnings were not realized. The shrimp and fish catches were healthy and apparently unaffected by the polluted water. One expert suggested that Hurricane Dennis was the reason. When Dennis had saturated the soils and almost flooded the rivers a few weeks earlier, large amounts of freshwater had come pouring out of the Neuse's mouth, sending the salt-loving shrimp and fish fleeing so that they were elsewhere when the polluted water arrived.

GLOBAL WARMING AND HURRICANES

In most tropical oceans, sea-surface temperatures have been rising steadily for several decades. Long-term global warming and the resultant rise in seawater temperatures could mean more frequent tropical cyclones of greater intensity occurring in more places around the world. A cyclone's main fuel is the warm water it pulls up as it hovers above the ocean. As the water vapor rises, cools, and condenses, it adds energy to the winds. Another result of a warmer world is sea-level rise, which could lead to higher storm surges and damage farther inland. Whether the ocean temperature changes are due to human-caused global warming or part of a broader trend, the link between hurricane intensity and warmer water is well established.

Mitch: Mountain Mover

Areas affected by Hurricane Mitch. The category 5 storm was the deadliest hurricane in the Western Hemisphere since 1780, killing some 9,000 people in Central America. Its rains and wind caused over $5 billion in damage.

Guatemala

Human Toll:
258 Deaths
120 Missing
105,700 Affected

Infrastructure Damage:
98 Bridges Destroyed
60% of Roads Impacted

Honduras

Human Toll:
6,600 Deaths
8,052 Missing
2,100,000 Affected

Infrastructure Damage:
170 Bridges Destroyed
70% of Roads Impacted

CARIBBEAN SEA

Belmopan
Belize

Guatemala

Guatemala City

San Salvador
El Salvador

Honduras

Tegucigalpa

Nicaragua

Nicaragua

Human Toll:
2,055 Deaths
1,084 Missing
868,000 Affected

Infrastructure Damage:
71 Bridges Destroyed
70% of Roads Impacted

El Salvador

Human Toll:
239 Deaths
135 Missing
84,000 Affected

Infrastructure Damage:
17 Bridges Destroyed
20% of Roads Impacted

Managua

Costa Rica

San José

NORTH PACIFIC OCEAN

Impacts on Agriculture

Nicaragua – 30% of Banana Crop Destroyed
Guatemala – 45–60% of Corn Crop Destroyed
Honduras – 90% of Banana Crop Destroyed

Entire villages were wiped off the map by the wrath of Hurricane Mitch. While Mitch was not a strong hurricane when it hit Honduras and Nicaragua in late October of 1998, it stalled for a week, soaking the area. The storm dumped an estimated 50 to 75 inches (127–190 cm) of water onto mountainsides already saturated by the rainy season. It was more than the mountains could take.

The sides of the mountains, composed of loosely packed volcanic soil, had been developed without foresight or good engineering. This made them vulnerable to erosion. In many places the slopes simply fell. An estimated 11,000 people died in the mudslides and floods.

Twice as many were listed as missing after the storm, and as many as one million were left homeless. It was the second deadliest hurricane in recorded human history.

The Huddled Masses

Many of the victims were the poorest of their countries, living in overcrowded conditions in river valleys and on hillsides. The land they inhabited had long been deforested, leaving few trees to hold the wet soil in place.

Tropical storm Mitch was born on October 22 out of a tropical depression in the southern Caribbean. On October 23 and 24, it drifted north, gaining speed and stature. On October 26 it became a category 5 hurricane. For two days it lessened in intensity and drifted next to Honduras, dousing that country and Nicaragua with rain and waves reaching 40 to 50 feet (12–15 m) high.

Then the hurricane moved inland, slowly winding through the mountains and giving off still more rain. The rain filled the cone of the dormant Casita volcano in Nicaragua. On October 30, the side of the cone broke, burying the villages below.

Similarly, above the Honduran capital of Tegucigalpa, the Choluteca River held a large amount of water behind a temporary dam made of debris. The mayor, Cesar Castellanos, warned the town and then went to survey the lake. He died on November 1 in a helicopter crash. As predicted, the Choluteca River flooded the city.

The tragic numbers of dead and missing were daunting, and the amount of money it would take to rebuild was equally unbelievable— $5 billion in infrastructure was destroyed. Roads, bulldozers, bridges, tractors, and basic housing and food were all things these cash-strapped countries could scarcely afford.

Flood damage along the Choluteca River in Tegucigalpa, Honduras. Mitch hit Honduras the hardest, killing 6,600 people, injuring 12,000, washing away entire villages, and destroying most of the nation's crops and infrastructure.

Road to Recovery

Even as people began to shovel out and address their losses, relief workers noticed a minor bright spot. For the most part, the refugees were not fighting diseases as they tried to put their lives back together. Often refugee camps are prime ground for cholera, dysentery, and other diseases found in unsanitary conditions. But U.S. Navy doctors found little evidence of the diseases. One reason was that many people had left the area to live with relatives instead of in crowded camps, and another is that water drained quickly from the mountains. Getting food to remote settings continued to be a problem, however, as roads, bridges, and even bulldozers were washed away.

Months passed as, slowly and painfully, the communities began to rebuild. But the residents went forward with new insight. "The positive aspect of Mitch is that it shook all of us,

SPECIFICATIONS

HURRICANE MITCH, 1998
Formed: October 22, 1998
Dissipated: November 5, 1998
Highest wind speed: 180 mph (290 km/h)
Lowest pressure: 905 mb
Damage: over $5 billion (1998 US$)
Deaths: 11,000–18,000 direct

awakened us to the fact that the world is changing, and we have to be part of the change," the Honduran minister of education, Ramon Calix Figueroa, told the *Christian Science Monitor* eight months after the storm.

Environmental groups also took a step forward. Spurred by the massive loss of life and housing, communities took an interest in better farming techniques and reforestation programs offered in both Nicaragua and Honduras.

While many local programs and organizations already existed, the practices of terraced farming and reforestation were not widespread enough

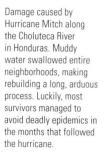

Damage caused by Hurricane Mitch along the Choluteca River in Honduras. Muddy water swallowed entire neighborhoods, making rebuilding a long, arduous process. Luckily, most survivors managed to avoid deadly epidemics in the months that followed the hurricane.

to curtail mudslides and other disasters. A year after the disaster, efficient wood-burning stoves were popular items, reducing the need for wood by two-thirds. And reforestation programs were catching on.

Others investigated better prediction, prevention, and evacuation plans. The lessons learned from events like Hurricane Mitch may not prevent natural hazards, but perhaps they can keep them from becoming disasters.

A family near El Progresso, Honduras, watches a river rise on October 28, 1998, two days after Hurricane Mitch reached its peak intensity. Even as it began to weaken, the storm unleashed downpours on Honduras that flooded 50 rivers. More than 150,000 Hondurans fled to higher ground, but many others, like this family, were trapped by the rising water.

NOT ALWAYS DISASTROUS

Hurricanes and the floods they bring are disastrous to the humans that live in their path. And at first glance, storms can be catastrophic for the wildlife as well. But like a fire or a volcanic eruption, hurricanes are part of the natural systems of the areas in which they occur. The winds and floods can act as a housecleaning—out with the old, in with the new.

While the storm devastates both habitat and wildlife, it creates opportunities for other types of plants and animals. Downed trees make it harder in the short term for some birds, but sunlight is able to reach new plant growth on the ground. Animals that eat the ground foliage, such as deer and some insects, and the animals that in turn eat the insects have a chance to flourish.

When a Hurricane Hit Galveston

The hurricane that struck Galveston, Texas, on September 8, 1900, and killed 8,000 people did not come without warning. But few took the warning seriously.

In 1900 Galveston considered itself the "Jewel of Texas." The island community of about 42,000 on the northwestern shore of the Gulf of Mexico boasted more money than Newport, Rhode Island, and compared its commercial activity to that of Wall Street. Beyond the boasts, the community was, by all accounts, thriving. It had a newspaper, schools, commerce, and churches.

What it did not have was a seawall, even though some residents complained they needed one. The beach was where people congregated on the weekends, so despite warnings in the

local paper that there was a hurricane offshore in the Gulf, many families walked the boardwalk to the wide sands and set up umbrellas and picnics for the day.

Unheeded Warning

Isaac Cline was the city's weather forecaster. He tracked the storm in the Gulf and used the newly instated telegraph to keep contact with the National Weather Bureau in Washington, D.C.

Wreckage left in Galveston, Texas, by the 1900 hurricane, the deadliest natural disaster ever to strike the United States. Storm surges flooded the island city up to 15 feet (4.6 m), demolishing one-third of its area and leaving no building undamaged. The hurricane killed a sixth of Galveston's population, so many that crews were forced to cremate victims still trapped in debris piles like this one.

"The water rose at a steady rate from 3 PM until about 7:30 PM, when there was a sudden rise of about 4 feet in as many seconds."

—ISAAC M. CLINE, THE UNITED STATES WEATHER BUREAU'S MONTHLY WEATHER REVIEW, SEPTEMBER 1900

When the storm veered off the Gulf and hit Louisiana on September 7, telegraph lines were damaged and Cline could not receive further storm reports. But he looked at the weather conditions, raised the hurricane warning flag, and put a note in the local paper. Early on the morning of September 8, few people in Galveston heeded the warning. They saw a few clouds and a few swells, but nothing remarkable, and continued with their day.

By 10:00 AM it was too late to run. The island was cut off as breakers smashed beach buildings, and extra water in Galveston Bay swamped the bridges that connected the island with the mainland.

At 2:30 PM Cline telegraphed Washington, "Gulf rising rapidly; half the city now under water; great loss of life must result."

That was the last message Cline was able to get out.

Nowhere to Run

By 5:00 PM, the water of Galveston Bay had met the water of the Gulf of Mexico, submerging the entire city. At 5:15, wind gusts were recorded at 100 miles per hour (161 km/h) just before the wind meter was destroyed. The town was being pulled apart. Roofs flew off. Chunks of buildings fell.

By 6:30, 10 feet (3 m) of water surged into the streets. People swam out of their houses looking for a safe place. The water continued to climb, and wind speed increased.

One family got in their boat and pulled in as many swimmers as they could. The Duncan family was credited with saving 200 people that night. Isaac Cline survived, but his wife did not.

As the water receded, Galveston found it had lost about 8,000 residents, and thousands of homes. The streets were clogged with the bloated bodies of family and friends as well as animals and debris. Individual burial was impossible. Some parts of the town tried taking the bodies to sea and dumping them, but to their horror the bodies floated back. Funeral pyres were set up and the workers were given whiskey to get through the grim task of burning their own dead family members.

Galveston looked at the losses and built a seawall. When another hurricane hit in 1915, the seawall held and only eight people died.

A house on Galveston's Avenue N ripped from its foundation by floodwaters. At its highest point, Galveston rose only 8 feet (2.4 m) above sea level, and the entire city was submerged during the hurricane. Despite its devastation, Galveston was self-sufficient again within six months, thanks in part to $1,258,000 in donations.

Other Major Storms

When the Bhola cyclone hit East Pakistan (now Bangladesh) on November 13, 1970, it killed between 300,000 and 500,000 people. The cyclone started its approach on the night of November 12, easing into the Bay of Bengal. The bay borders one of the most fertile parts of the world, an area that is densely populated and very flat. The shoreline offers almost no natural defense, and few in the poor country could afford to build hurricane-proof houses.

In the early hours of the morning, the winds of the Bhola cyclone made landfall, destroying houses in the way. The storm surge that followed, at 15 to 20 feet (5 to 6 m), wiped out much of what was left. Many people drowned in their sleep. The greatest destruction and highest loss of life occurred on the islands in the Ganges Delta, south of Dhaka. While the true number of dead will probably never be known, the Bhola cyclone can surely be counted as one of the worst natural disasters of all time.

After the disaster, the people of the area were outraged over the Pakistani government's slow response time. The government response was a major factor in the Bangladesh Liberation War in 1971.

Survivors in Manpura, East Pakistan (now Bangladesh), survey the effects of the deadliest hurricane on record. Many villagers were swept from their beds by a storm surge measuring 15 to 20 feet (4.5–6 m) in the early morning hours of November 13, 1970. Here, the remnants of tin-roofed homes stand as a testament to the hurricane's destruction.

SPECIFICATIONS

BHOLA, 1970
Formed: November 7, 1970
Dissipated: November 13, 1970
Highest wind speed: 120 mph (190 km/h)
Lowest pressure: unknown
Damage: unknown
Deaths: up to 500,000 direct

> "Good God! What horror and destruction . . . the ear-piercing shrieks of the distressed were sufficient to strike astonishment into angels."
>
> —ALEXANDER HAMILTON
> ON THE HURRICANE OF AUGUST 31, 1772

SPECIFICATIONS

GREAT HURRICANE OF 1780
Formed: October 10, 1780 (est.)
Dissipated: October 19, 1780 (est.)
Deaths: up to 22,000 direct

An English trade ship in the channel at the entrance to Havana, c. 1777.

The Great Hurricane of 1780

It was the deadliest Atlantic hurricane of all time, and may have changed the history of the United States.

In October 1780 British warships were sailing to fight the French for control of the area around the Antilles Islands and to fight the rebellious American colonists for control of the coast. As the British warships moved through Barbados they were caught in a gigantic hurricane.

The hurricane did more than just blow through the region; it crushed it. On October 10, Barbados had a bright orange sunset followed by light rain. At 10:00 PM the winds had reached hurricane strength. For the next several days the hurricane stopped over the islands.

"The strongest buildings and the whole houses, most of which were stone and remarkable for their solidity, gave way to the fury of the wind, and were torn up to their foundations; all the forts destroyed, and many of the heavy cannon carried upwards of

a hundred feet from the forts," wrote Sir George Rodney to Lady Rodney on December 10, 1780. "More than 6,000 perished and all the inhabitants are entirely ruined."

Among those that perished were British sailors and warships. Eight of the twelve warships sank and their sailors drowned, a loss that ultimately benefited the American colonists in their fight for independence.

While records are not conclusive, it is estimated that the giant hurricane killed at least 22,000 people on Barbados, St. Lucia, St. Vincent, Martinique, Hispaniola, and Puerto Rico, before passing south of Bermuda on October 18.

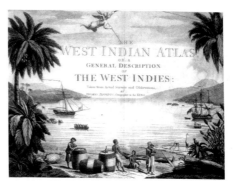

An English sailor, accompanied by local inhabitants, enjoys a West Indian beach in this 1775 scene from a British atlas. The waters look peaceful here, but five years later, eight of Britain's warships would sink in the Caribbean during the hurricane that is still counted as the Atlantic Ocean's deadliest.

EXTREME NATURAL DISASTERS

CHAPTER 2

TORNADOES

TORNADOES HAVE the fastest and strongest winds of any type of storm—and with that speed comes great power. Scientists have clocked winds at 315 miles per hour (507 km/h), which is faster than any recorded hurricane winds. The most intense twisters are capable of lifting a house off its foundation, tossing it across town, and sweeping the remaining concrete clean.

Tornadoes are short-lived storms, lasting only 30 minutes on average, and measuring only about a quarter mile (0.4 km) across. But as people in the American Midwest can testify, tornadoes often come as a surprise, and their force should always be taken seriously.

Tornadoes originate with thunderstorms, though not every thunderstorm becomes a tornado. Thunderstorms arise when cool air meets with warm, moist air. In order for a tornado to form, two tiers of wind must be present. The two tiers, located in the upper and lower atmosphere, travel in opposite directions and at different speeds. Scientists speculate that when the two winds interact, they somehow form a horizontal, spinning tube of air that is tilted up by updrafts.

These huge spinning winds, called mesocyclones, can reach 10 miles (16 km) into the air. As the clouds turn, they act like vacuums sucking up more warm air, which turns into more energy. Usually it is a mesocyclone that spawns a tornado.

Left: This storm was photographed south of Dimmit, Texas, on June 2, 1995. Tornadoes can generate the strongest winds known on Earth, and when they strike populated areas, they can cause destruction of property and great loss of life. Inset: Uprooted trees and a demolished home lie in mute testament to the power of a tornado that swept through Kentucky in 2005.

Right: A tornado looms over rural Nebraska. Tornadoes range from as narrow as a few feet to more than two miles wide, but larger size does not necessarily equal more power. Tornadoes can intensify as they tighten and inflict severe damage, while larger funnels might have little effect on the landscape.

What triggers a tornado still is not completely understood, but here is what scientists believe happens: A spinning cloud, heavy with moisture, begins to hang down below the rest of a storm. This is the funnel cloud. As the funnel gets narrower and narrower, it spins even faster. When it touches down, it is called a tornado.

Tornadoes often look like long funnels, but they can also be shaped like a barrel, with the top and bottom equal in size. They are sometimes completely obscured by rain or dust, which can make them difficult to detect.

Tornadoes are gray and white to start with, the color of the clouds that form them. But as they touch the ground and pull up soil, they change color. The funnel from Texas will match the brown dirt found there. Or a tornado might pick up dirt and carry it across country, so the red soil of Oklahoma can be seen spinning in Kansas.

Below: Tornado Alley. Although tornadoes strike all over the world, from New Zealand to Africa to Europe, hundreds blow through the American Great Plains every year. Cold, dry air from Canada and warm, moist air from the Gulf of Mexico are able to flow unimpeded over the flat land in the region, where they meet to spawn twisters.

Tornadoes have been seen on every continent except Antarctica, but they are most common in areas where there is an abundance of warm, moist air near the ground.

Geography of Tornadoes

While tornadoes can happen nearly anywhere, a section of the Great Plains in the United States has been dubbed Tornado Alley. This area covers parts of northern Texas, Oklahoma, Nebraska, Kansas, Iowa, and Missouri. With the Rocky Mountains on the west, the Gulf of Mexico on the south, and thousands

"Tornado Alley"

Minnesota
S. Dakota
Nebraska Iowa
Colorado Kansas
Oklahoma
Texas

of uninterrupted acres for the winds to roar through, this area has the meteorological ingredients necessary to cook up hundreds of twisters every year. Warm, moist air blows in from the Gulf of Mexico and mixes with dry air coming off the Rockies. Pressure builds and a thunderstorm 50,000 feet (15,240 m) tall can form in only a few minutes, which may generate a tornado.

TORNADO RATINGS

The National Weather Service uses the Fujita scale to classify tornadoes. This scale rates tornadoes from 0 to 5 based on the amount and type of wind damage.

RANK	WIND SPEED	STRENGTH	DAMAGE	DESCRIPTION OF DAMAGE
F-0	40 to 72 mph (64–116 km/h)	Weak	Light	Some damage to chimneys; branches broken off trees; shallow-rooted trees pushed over; signboards damaged
F-1	73 to 112 mph (117–180 km/h)	Weak	Moderate	Peels surface off roofs; mobile homes pushed off foundations or overturned; moving autos blown off road
F-2	113 to 157 mph (181–253 km/h)	Strong	Considerable	Roofs torn off frame houses; mobile homes demolished; railroad boxcars overturned; large trees snapped or uprooted; light-object missiles generated; cars lifted off ground
F-3	158 to 206 mph (254–332 km/h)	Strong	Severe	Roofs and some walls torn off well-constructed houses; trains overturned; trees uprooted; heavy cars lifted off ground and thrown
F-4	207 to 260 mph (333–418 km/h)	Violent	Devastating	Well-constructed houses leveled; structures with weak foundations blown off some distance; cars thrown and large-object missiles generated
F-5	261 mph (419 km/h) and above	Violent	Incredibly violent	Strong frame houses lifted off foundations and swept away; automobile-size missiles fly through the air in excess of 100 meters (109 yards); trees debarked; incredible phenomena can occur

Bangladesh: Worst in History

April, May, and June are dangerous months in Bangladesh, when oncoming monsoons can breed tornadoes. Here, residents of Rampur, about 45 minutes north of Dhaka, walk through what remains of their village on May 14, 1996. The previous afternoon, a tornado with winds of 125 miles per hour (201 km/h) had devastated the northern part of the country.

Tornado warning systems exist in many countries, but the unpredictable nature of tornadoes makes early alerts difficult to execute. Even those who are tuned in at the right time to hear the information may get only 10 minutes' notice to seek cover. And in many parts of the world, there is no warning at all.

On April 27, 1989, Bangladesh suffered the worst tornado disaster in history. The country was in the midst of a drought, and the rice crop was at risk. Just hours before the tornado arrived, Bangladesh's president, H. M. Ershad, had ordered national prayers for rain. The rain came, and with it the wind. That evening, a tornado

SPECIFICATIONS

BANGLADESH, 1989
Date: April 26, 1989
Rank: unrated, but from level of destruction, considered an F-5
Damages: 80,000 homeless and 12,000 injured
Deaths: 1,300
Areas affected: Manikgaj district of Bangladesh
Path extent: 10 miles long, 1 mile wide
Wind speed: 100 mph (161 km/h)

registering winds at 100 miles per hour (161 km/h) tore into the heavily populated Manikgaj district, 25 miles (40.2 km) north of Dhaka, the capital city. Village after village gave way to the swirling storm.

SPECIFICATIONS

BANGLADESH, 1996
Date: May 1996
Damages: 50,000 injured
Deaths: 500
Wind speed: 125 mph (201 km/h)

With no warning system and flimsily constructed houses, the funnel cloud lifted people, houses, and animals into the air as it whipped through 20 villages. "I saw black clouds gathering in the sky," said eyewitness Sayeda Begum. "In moments we found we were flying along with the house." Begum, her husband, and four children landed safely, but their village of 10,000, Saturia, was destroyed.

The 1989 tornado killed more than 1,000 people, injured 12,000, and left 80,000 homeless.

Stricken Again

In May 1996 tornadoes tore through the low-lying country again, killing 500 and injuring another 50,000. Buildings were torn apart, their roofs becoming shrapnel hurtling out of the 125 mile per hour (201 km/h) wind. Humans were tossed and broken like dolls. Trees turned upside down so that their roots provided shade for the dazed survivors. Hospitals and relief workers were overwhelmed by the tragedy.

Tornadoes often threaten Bangladesh in April, May, and June as the weather system builds to the annual July monsoon.

Residents of Rampur, Bangladesh, mourn the victims of the May 13, 1996, tornado. Lasting only 20 minutes, the cyclone killed 500 people and injured 50,000.

TORNADOES AROUND THE WORLD

The United States records over a thousand tornadoes a year, by far the most of any country on Earth. This is mostly due to the climate conditions in the Great Plains, but it is also a result of the tornado recording technology used in the United States.

In the rest of the world, approximately 300 tornadoes are reported each year. Bangladesh and East India often have severe thunderstorms that turn deadly with tornadoes, and Scandinavia, Italy, Spain, and the United Kingdom all report as many as 30 twisters a year. In the Southern Hemisphere, Australia, Argentina, Uruguay, Brazil, and South Africa report significant numbers.

Other countries, including Russia and China, are only beginning to report their weather disasters. In 1984 Moscow faced an F-5 tornado and no one outside the country knew about it. As more scientists agree to make data public, it may be discovered that there are other tornado hotbeds in the world.

The Tri-State Tornado

SPECIFICATIONS

TRI-STATE TORNADO OUTBREAK, 1925
Date: March 18, 1925
Duration of storm: 5 hours
Maximum-ranked tornado: F-5
Damages: $1.65 billion (2005 US$)
Deaths: 625 from one tornado; 747 from all
  tornadoes that day
Path extent: 219 miles (352 km)

March 18, 1925, was a Wednesday, a regular school day for many children in the southern regions of Illinois, Missouri, and Indiana. In Murphysboro, Illinois, the elementary school principal suddenly announced that everyone had to get to the basement. Everyone in the building headed downstairs as the sky turned black and dangerous-looking clouds quickly approached. As the children took cover, an F-5 category twister tore through the town, blasting the school's glass windows above them. They were safe, but many of their parents were not. In less than an hour, 541 people were killed in Murphysboro and the neighboring towns of Gorham, West Frankfort, and Parrish. The total death count was 625 along the tornado's 219-mile (352 km) path.

The strip of destruction had begun in Ellington, Missouri, at 1:01 PM.

There was no warning system in place, so no one had known it was coming. And even those who saw the tornado could not identify it as such. Witnesses described it as a "rolling fog." It did not have the traditional funnel or even barrel shape but appeared as a massive cloud near the ground. Leaving Ellington, the tornado moved north at more than 70 miles per hour (113 km/h), wiping out houses in the town of Annapolis and killing four people.

Longfellow School in Murphysboro, Illinois, destroyed by the Tri-State tornado. Seventeen children were killed, bringing the town's death toll to 234. The twister leveled three-quarters of the town, aided by widespread fires that could not be extinguished because the storm had damaged the water supply.

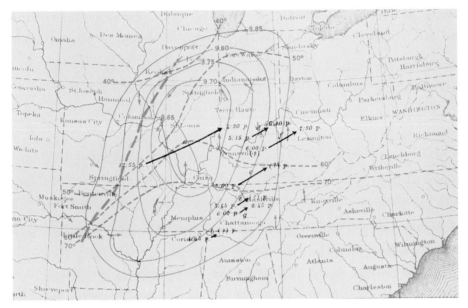

Left: An April 1925 map of the area struck by the Tri-State tornado. The long black line shows the storm's track: 219 miles (352 km), the longest of any recorded tornado.

Below: An engineering committee in southern Illinois examines a plank impaled by a board during the Tri-State tornado. The storm spent over two hours in Illinois, where it killed 600 people and all but demolished five towns.

Across the Mississippi

Crossing the Mississippi into Illinois at about 2:30, the tornado hit the town of Gorham. "The walls seemed to fall in all around us," one child wrote about her experience in the school, an account that was later published in *Acts of God: The Old Farmer's Almanac Unpredictable Guide to Weather and Natural Disasters*. "Then the floor at one end of the building gave way. We all slipped or slid in that direction. If it hadn't been for the seats it would have been like sliding down a cellar door."

Gorham was destroyed. Almost half the 500 residents were dead or injured, and only 20 of the town's 80 houses were left standing.

"The air was filled with 10,000 things," The *St. Louis Post-Dispatch* reported two days after the Tri-State tornado. "Boards, poles, cans, garments, stoves, whole sides of the little frame houses, in some cases the houses themselves, were picked up and smashed to Earth." Here, an overturned house lies more than 50 feet from its foundation, in Griffin, Indiana. In the 400-person town, the tornado killed 54 and injured 200.

Moving on to Murphysboro, the tornado accelerated to 73 miles per hour (117 km/h). It leveled 150 of the town's 200 blocks and killed 234 residents. All over town, fires broke out that could not be extinguished, since the tornado had also knocked out the water supply.

In West Frankfort, 148 people were killed and 410 injured, numbers that would have been higher except that many of the men were working underground in the mines. The *St. Louis Post-Dispatch* wrote, "Only a dozen houses remain standing and 11 of these are damaged with roofs and porches missing. Piles of bricks and timbers fill the streets, trees are split and uprooted. The scene resembles that of a world-war battlefield, except that on a battlefield the victims are men. Here they are mostly women and children."

The tornado kept moving, destroying the town of Parrish, Illinois, before crossing the Wabash River into Indiana. In the border town of Griffin, 25 people were killed. Finally, outside of Petersburg, Indiana, the winds stopped. After more than three hours and 219 miles (352 km), the tornado dissipated. It was the tornado with the longest continuous contact with the ground in United States history. On the same day, other tornadoes occurred in Kentucky and Tennessee, killing another 52 people, bringing the day's death toll to 747.

The damage that day was estimated at $16.5 million, which in today's currency would be closer to $1.65 billion.

RAINING FROGS

As a tornado or waterspout goes over the top of a body of water, frogs, fish, and nearby birds may be pulled up into the vortex. They may come down quickly or be dropped miles away as part of another storm. Sometimes the animals are transported unharmed and descend gently from the sky, but more often the experience kills them. In March 1998, frogs rained down on Croydon, England, and in August 2000, fish fell out of the sky in Great Yarmouth, England. The sprats were dead but still fresh, suggesting they had been picked up recently by an ocean tornado. Animals are sometimes frozen solid when they fall from the sky, suggesting that they were pulled up to the upper atmosphere before returning to Earth. The journal *Nature* reported on a gopher turtle completely encased in ice that fell in Vicksburg, Mississippi, during a hailstorm.

When a tornado funnel touches down on a body of water, it can pick up spray and form what is known as a waterspout.

Moore, Oklahoma: Three Times the Devastation

M oore, Oklahoma, is located in the heart of Tornado Alley. The state of Oklahoma records hundreds of tornadoes a year. Most of them cause little damage because they are not major storms and they occur out on the prairie. The National Oceanic and Atmospheric Administration (NOAA) records these funnel clouds by longitude and latitude, since there are no towns in the vicinity of the events.

Moore, on the other hand, is a suburb of sprawling Oklahoma City. As urban areas cover more territory, more people and property are in the path of tornadoes, and so the tally of damage increases.

A category F-3 storm photographed on May 3, 1999, south of Anadarko in west-central Oklahoma. This tornado preceded the F-5 behemoth that killed 48 people and caused $1.5 billion in damages across a 70-mile (112 km) swath of Oklahoma later that day.

SPECIFICATIONS

MOORE, OKLAHOMA, 1999
Date: May 3, 1999
Duration of storm: 72 hours
Maximum-ranked tornado: F-5
Number of tornadoes: 66
Damages: $1.5 billion
Deaths: 48
Tornado path extent: 70 miles (113 km)
Maximum wind speed: 318 mph (512 km/h)

Cars pummeled and tossed by the tornado's winds, which reached a maximum speed of 318 miles per hour (512 km/h).

Two Twisters in One Year

On June 13, 1998, a moderate tornado struck Oklahoma City. No one was killed, and building damage was estimated at only $300,000. Unfortunately, the storm of May 3, 1999, was less docile.

"It started as multiple funnels that danced around each other," helicopter pilot Jim Gardner told *Newsweek* magazine. Gardner watched the storm from the air, from about a mile away. "All of a sudden the dance got tight and they converged into one." Gardner was watching what turned out to be one of the strongest tornadoes on record, a category F-5 on the Fujita scale. With wind speeds at a record-breaking 318 miles per hour (512 km/h), the half-mile-wide (0.8 km) funnel simply blew aside everything in its way, cutting a 70-mile (113 km) path of destruction across Oklahoma.

All afternoon, radio stations had announced thunderstorm warnings and then sounded sirens as the funnels appeared around 5 PM. NOAA recorded the gigantic funnel touching down at 5:26. Normally tornado funnels stay on the ground for only a few minutes, but this one held on to the dirt and trees of Oklahoma for over 90 minutes.

Neighborhoods were leveled. Marty Bernich told *Time* magazine that his family of four had huddled together in their utility room and were lifted into the air. All four of them survived, landing in their own yard. Their plan for rebuilding included a storm cellar.

Hit Again

On the night of May 3, 2003, a tornado classified as a slightly less powerful F-4 came through the same area. Sirens and radio and television announcements warned residents to take cover. Winds reached 200 miles per hour (322 km/h), snapping utility poles like toothpicks, breaking houses down or picking them up and shaking their contents across the state. Downed wires cluttered major roads, and airports lost as many as 75 planes to wind damage.

An F-1 tornado reaches for the ground between Verden and Chickasha in west-central Oklahoma on May 3, 1999. This storm would produce at least two more tornadoes that day, both of which struck populated areas.

SPECIFICATIONS

MOORE, OKLAHOMA, 2003
Date: May 3, 2003
Maximum-ranked tornado: F-4
Damages: $130 million, 110 injured
Deaths: 40
Maximum wind speed: 200 mph (322 km/h)

As the funnel touched down at random, it flattened some houses while taking just a few shingles from others. From Oklahoma City to Tulsa, over 40 people were killed, 110 injured, and

damage upward of $130 million was caused. President Bush declared the region a federal disaster area, which allowed the cities to apply for federal relief funds. The money helped many to rebuild—until next time.

The day after the storm, an Oklahoma couple surveys the wreckage of one of the 1,500 houses destroyed in the state during the tornado's 90 minutes on the ground.

IMPROVING THE WARNING SYSTEMS

In the tornado-busy Great Plains region, Doppler radar equipment is used to predict severe weather. The radar systems are posted at approximately 100-mile (160 km) intervals, which leaves a lot of area uncovered where tornadoes might develop and even touch down without warning. Meteorologists hope to cut down on the gaps by installing smaller weather radars on cell-phone towers, about 20 miles (32 km) apart. This storm surveillance system could increase warning time to as much as 30 minutes. Other scientists are working on computer models that will help meteorologists predict which storms might develop into tornadoes and which will simply bring rain.

But the best defense is to know what a tornado looks and sounds like. Warning signs of a coming tornado are a dark, often greenish sky, a wall cloud, large hail, or a loud roar, similar to the sound of a freight train. Anyone witnessing any or all of these should take cover.

Palm Sunday Tornado Outbreak of 1965

Five states, 78 tornadoes, and 475 miles (764 km). The Palm Sunday tornado outbreak affected Iowa, Illinois, Indiana, Michigan, and Ohio with little or no warning, tearing apart houses, churches, and shopping malls.

The predicted weather for most of the area that day was unseasonably warm with a chance of showers in the evening, so the isolated tornadoes and thunderstorms came as a surprise. Unfortunately, radar tracking systems were scarce in 1965, and the warning system failed in many places due to technical difficulties, such as blown fuses or power outages.

Twelve Hours of Destruction

At about 1 PM, the first tornado was spotted in Clinton, Iowa. It was a devastating category F-4. A radio announcer in Cedar Rapids saw the funnel on his station's radar screen and alerted the local branch of the National Weather Service. The service did not yet have radar, but thanks to the announcer they were on the lookout for a storm.

As the storm moved eastward, another F-4 tornado appeared in Crystal Lake, Illinois, killing six people, destroying 145 homes, and damaging a junior high school. But it was northern Indiana that took the brunt of the tornadoes that day when several category F-4 and F-5 twisters touched down in the region.

Without a good warning system, many people were out enjoying the warm day at Lake Michigan when the thunderstorms started. Elkhart

Twin funnels bear down on Elkhart, Indiana, on Palm Sunday, April 11, 1965. Seventy-eight tornadoes rampaged over five Midwestern states that day.

in particular was hit hard. As college student James K. Sommers drove west on the Indiana Toll Road toward Elkhart, conditions worsened, bringing golf ball–size hail, so Sommers took cover under an overpass. The tornado hit ground nearby and blasted debris at the car. Sommers decided to stay put, knowing that sometimes tornadoes often come more than one at a time. As he waited, the person who had stopped behind him drove off. "He was struck by another tornado just two minutes later. His car along with several others was picked up and tossed like a toy into a barren cornfield on the north side of the Toll Road," said Sommers.

The storm and its tornadoes continued on to towns in Michigan and Ohio. Several Michigan cities, including Lansing, discovered that their relay systems were not working. And once the power and phones went out, few places had emergency transmitters.

After 12 hours, the storm dissipated, leaving more than 1,200 injured in its path, as well as hundreds dead and hundreds of thousands of dollars' worth of damages.

A New Warning System

In the aftermath of the tragedy, weather forecasters realized that not only had the warning systems failed, partly due to technical difficulties, but that the public did not know the difference between a forecast and an alert. After this storm, the National Weather Service developed a system with two specific types of warning: the tornado watch, which means that tornadoes are likely, and the tornado warning, the alert that goes out that a tornado has been spotted.

On Easter Sunday morning, a week after the Palm Sunday tornadoes, 66-year-old Elam Smith sat in the wreckage of his Alto, Indiana, home. Several tornadoes had ripped through the area, destroying most of Alto.

KNOWING WHEN TO TAKE COVER

It is often difficult to tell when bad weather might turn dangerous. In the United States, the National Weather Service works to continuously update weather predictions. When conditions are right for a tornado or severe thunderstorm, meteorologists post a severe thunderstorm or tornado watch.

When weather service personnel actually see a severe thunderstorm or tornado via Doppler radar or other instruments, they issue a warning, advising listeners to take cover. Meteorologists use real-time weather observations—from satellites, weather stations, balloon packages, airplanes, wind profilers, and Doppler radar images—to track a storm's movements, hoping to spot the formation of a funnel cloud or even a tornado as it touches down.

La Plata, Maryland, 2002

While tornadoes in the United States are generally associated with the Great Plains region, under the right conditions they can occur anywhere. Most residents of La Plata, Maryland, never considered the possibility of a category F-4 tornado touching down in their midst. While a Victorian-era house stood up to the winds of April 28, 2002, losing part of its roof, its neighbors fell.

The house had already survived a tornado in 1926 that destroyed the school, killing 14 children. The children's bodies had been laid out in the Victorian house. "It's pretty painful, but the roots of the town are right here," house owner Sam Phillips told the *New York Times*. "There's a spirit here, and Ace and Lulu Creavett [the 1926 owners] would want us to rebuild."

Across the Potomac

The tornado of 2002 started as a supercell thunderstorm that originated in Ohio and Kentucky. It moved

A map of the La Plata tornado's path, showing the degrees of damage it inflicted along the way. Although far from Tornado Alley, La Plata and nearby communities in Maryland and Virginia suffered a combined $108 million in damages.

SPECIFICATIONS

LA PLATA, MARYLAND, 2002
Date: April 28, 2002
Maximum-ranked tornado: F-4
Damages: more than $100 million, 121 injured in Maryland; $8 million and 17 injuries in Virginia
Deaths: 3
Wind speed: 200 mph (322 km/h)

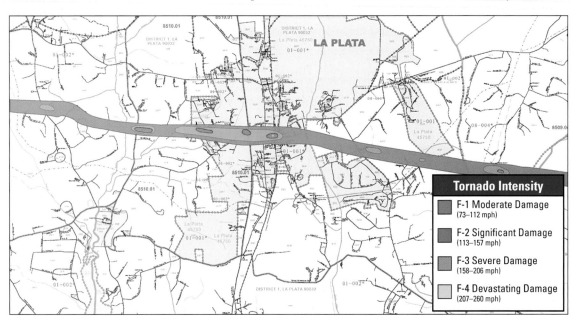

Tornado Intensity

F-1 Moderate Damage
(73–112 mph)

F-2 Significant Damage
(113–157 mph)

F-3 Severe Damage
(158–206 mph)

F-4 Devastating Damage
(207–260 mph)

"Tornadoes can kill at any strength,
and can strike anywhere."

—METEOROLOGIST JOHN OGREN OF THE NATIONAL WEATHER SERVICE

eastward, occasionally dropping a small funnel cloud but not doing any damage. Then it reached the Potomac River. The official NOAA report later stated that, "the storm rapidly changed its character as it crossed the Potomac River." The Potomac is over a half-mile (0.8 km) across at that point and tidal, which may be significant, but more research is required before a definite link can be made. Others conjectured that the storm increased in strength due to a warm front in La Plata. In either case, once the vicious storm crossed from Virginia into Maryland, rural Charles County was in its path.

Moving at 55 miles per hour (86 km/h), the storm took less than 10 minutes to travel from the river

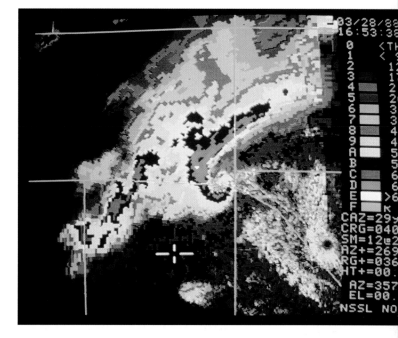

to the town center, leveling everything in its way. The water tower fell like a Tinkertoy. Power lines snapped. Tree bark vanished from trunks. Downtown, roofs and whole floors of buildings disappeared into the funnel. An orthodontist's office was destroyed as the tornado picked up wooden planks at the lumberyard and hurled them into the building. As in many storm events, it is not the wind that does the most damage, but the flying debris that it carries.

Above: A radar image of a hook echo in Norman, Oklahoma, in 1988. Hook echoes, curve-shaped signatures that occur when rain, hail, or debris spiral into the cyclone of a thunderstorm supercell, are often precursors to tornadoes.

Left: A "Doppler on Wheels" radar truck scans an Oklahoma thunderstorm. After the La Plata tornado, NOAA praised the Baltimore forecast office for its prestorm prediction and planning. They had been able to pinpoint, within a few hours, when the twister would hit.

Multiple Vortex

The tornado that hit La Plata had more than one funnel. During their investigation, NOAA researchers heard accounts of tornadoes occurring on opposite sides of town, which led them to believe that this was a multivortex tornado. In this phenomenon, more than one funnel circulates around the parent tornado's circulation.

La Plata is in one of the least populated parts of Maryland. If the tornado had started out farther north, things could have been much worse. La Plata is only about 25 miles (40 km) south of Washington, D.C.

Heading southeast from La Plata, the tornado made a close call with the Calvert Cliffs nuclear power plant in Lusby, Maryland. With winds over 200 miles an hour (322 km/h), the

Right: A satellite photo of a portion of the 2002 twister's path. The brown stripe of flattened vegetation leads from La Plata (at left) eastward toward the Patuxent River (beyond the edge of the image). With 260 mile per hour (418 km/h) winds, the tornado was the strongest ever recorded in Maryland.

Below: A tornado rages across farmland near Manchester, South Dakota, in June 2003. This storm, like the one that struck La Plata in 2002, was a multivortex tornado, meaning more than one funnel—usually between two and five—rotates around the larger center. The additional vortices can boost the system's wind speeds by 100 miles per hour and often leave swaths of severe devastation alongside relatively undamaged areas.

tornado certainly would have caused damage, but as it was, it passed a mere mile from the plant's concrete and steel walls. Engineers watched and pointed as the funnel moved out into Chesapeake Bay.

Rating the Storm

In the aftermath, scientists initially logged the tornado as an F-5, the most powerful level of tornado. But after further investigation, researchers decided much of the damage was caused by flying debris. An F-5 storm does more than just knock down trees and houses—it sweeps them away. La Plata had pile after pile of rubbish left behind, which indicated that this event was a level F-4 tornado.

Only 2 percent of all tornadoes are either level F-5 or F-4, but that percentage causes almost 70 percent of the damage seen every year. In La Plata, three people lost their lives and over 120 were injured. Eighty homes were destroyed, and several thousand were damaged. Seventy-five percent of the businesses in the downtown area were destroyed, and the total damage was estimated at more than $100 million. The state of Maryland declared La Plata a disaster area, and neighbors from around the state arrived to help clean up. The Victorian house was rebuilt and may well withstand another storm or two.

A Hoisington, Kansas, home after an encounter with an F-4 tornado.

SAFE FROM THE WIND

The safest place to be during a tornado is underground, in a basement or storm cellar. Unfortunately, many new homes are built without basements, even in Tornado Alley. In such a case, experts suggest going to a solid room at the center of the house, like a bathroom, and protecting yourself from falling debris with a mattress or something else. Those living in mobile homes should go as quickly as possible to a storm shelter. Mobile homes are generally lined up in a row, and when one goes, the others are likely to follow.

CHAPTER 3

ICE STORMS, SNOWSTORMS, AND AVALANCHES

UNDER THE RIGHT CIRCUMSTANCES, snow and ice can turn a mundane landscape into a shimmering snow globe, bejeweling eaves and branches with dangling tinsel, blanketing parking lots and muddy fields with a romantic glaze of glittering white. But that beauty, in excess, can be deadly. What looks like a winter wonderland might actually be a disaster area.

Ice takes on many guises. A storm might inflict freezing rain: water droplets that fall through a shallow layer of cold air but do not freeze until they hit the ground. If the cold layer is slightly deeper, the raindrops solidify in midair into ice pellets, or sleet. Snowflakes—six-sided ice crystals—tend to form higher in the atmosphere, when water vapor skips the liquid phase and changes straight into a solid. A snowstorm qualifies as a blizzard if precipitation limits visibility to a quarter of a mile (0.4 km) or less and the wind is blowing at least 35 miles per hour (56 km/h) for three hours or more.

Left: A snowstorm can bring joy to the hearts of skiers and school-children who yearn for a "snow day," but excessive snowfall can lead to hazardous road conditions and damage to trees and buildings. Inset: Although all snowflakes are hexagonal, it is probably true that no two are exactly alike.

Background: Driving in snow can be harrowing, even for experienced drivers.

Below: An avalanche occurs when a mass of material breaks free from its surroundings and slides down a slope, collecting additional material on its way. Snow avalanches are fairly common in mountainous areas and are sometimes caused by people engaging in various snow sports, such as climbing, skiing, and snowmobiling.

Ice storms and blizzards are winter's hallmarks; hail, on the other hand, tends to strike in spring. Hailstones—lumps of ice at least 0.2 inches (0.5 cm) in diameter—form inside thunderclouds, rather than freezing as they fall, like sleet. And from high up in the mountains, avalanches are a threat all year, in the form of masses of ice, snow, and debris that career down the slopes. Avalanches can be dislodged by anything from earthquakes to loud-voiced skiers, and once they start rolling, at speeds greater than the winds of a force-5 hurricane and up to several miles wide, they can prove impossible to outrun.

In each disaster, the main ingredient is the same—frozen water—but each destroys in its own particular way. An individual hailstone might not seem dangerous, but thousands of them plummeting from the sky can reduce a city to a crisis zone in minutes. Avalanches hurl tons of snow—and often rocks and fallen trees—at their victims, smothering what they fail to crush outright. Falling snow builds up little by little until it chokes off roads and runways and its weight threatens trees and buildings. Ice quickly makes roads hazardous, and causes power lines to fall, leaving thousands without electricity for days.

A pedestrian fights against the wind on a street in Rochester, Minnesota, during a blizzard on March 24, 1966. The city's average annual snowfall has been estimated at 48.9 inches (124.2 cm).

As always, prediction and preparation are key to minimizing the effects of these catastrophes. But what happens when forecasts are too late, too vague, or ignored? Worse yet, what becomes of the population when warning is impossible?

Warning Systems

The Smithsonian Institution played a central role in early understanding of weather patterns in the United States. In the 1850s the Smithsonian collected weather reports from hundreds of telegraph stations. This observation network led to the creation of the National Weather Bureau. In the years since, advances in meteorology and communication have improved both the accuracy of forecasts and how quickly the public can be warned about severe storms.

Warning systems proliferated in the 1960s. Radar technology developed during World War II helped meteorologists locate potentially dangerous storms, and thousands of communities set up alarm sirens. In 1963 the Federal Communications Commission established the Emergency Broadcast System to alert the nation in case of a civil-defense emergency; local offices of the National Weather Service were also permitted to use the system. Today, the National Weather Service issues a blizzard warning whenever it expects heavy snow with winds of 35 miles (56.3 km) per hour or more to continue for at least three hours. Local media, emergency management, law enforcement, and government agencies then announce the warnings to the public.

The Ice Storm of 1998

Opposite page: The St. Lawrence River in winter. Inhabitants of the region surrounding the river are accustomed to severe winter weather, but the 1998 storm was extreme. In Canada, the storm affected more people than any previous weather event in Canadian history.

Below: This map shows the extent of the 1998 ice storm, which affected parts of Ontario, Quebec, and New Brunswick in Canada and the states of New York, Vermont, New Hampshire, and Maine. Freezing rain accumulations ranged from 1.6 to 3.9 inches (40 to 100 mm).

A round the St. Lawrence River, winter storms are par for the course. Gray skies start dumping snow and ice in October and continue until April, but the natives are ready. Veteran fleets of plows keep the roads open, the school buses run on time, and stout power lines stand up against winter's worst. To a population so used to the cold, only the most extreme winter weather can disturb their routine.

Every once in a while, though, the right combination of circumstances creates disaster. In the first days of 1998, a stream of warm, moist air from the Gulf of Mexico collided east of the Great Lakes with very cold air from the Arctic. Most Gulf storms drift out to sea and die somewhere around Iceland, but in this case a large high-pressure system in Bermuda pushed the air current west of the usual course. Then

SPECIFICATIONS

THE ICE STORM OF 1998
Deaths: between 35 and 60
Damages: Canada—$3 billion, U.S.—$1.4 billion; 18 million acres (7.3 hectares) of forests damaged; more than 3 million people without power

the Arctic mass trapped it. As the less-dense warm air butted over the cold layer, raindrops descended through the nippy air below and chilled but did not quite harden. They hit the ground as a liquid, spread out into a slick, glassy lacquer, and then froze. Had it been a little warmer, it would have been normal rain; a little colder, and it would have snowed. Either would have been less calamitous for the people of the northeastern United States and southeastern Canada.

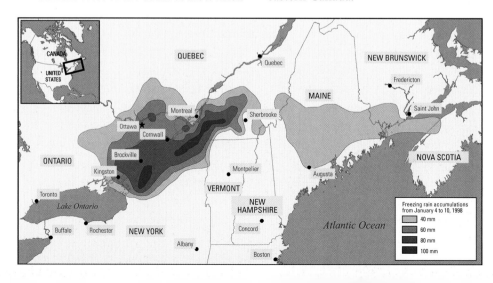

"Just because the sun is out, it ain't over."

—ANGUS KING, GOVERNOR OF MAINE, ON POWER OUTAGES

Millions Lose Power

The first freezing rain began to fall on January 4. Most northerners resigned themselves to a morning of windshield scraping. But the Gulf low-pressure system kept pumping a seemingly endless supply of wet air into the storm.

By January 8, when the precipitation finally stopped, Canada had endured 80 total hours of freezing rain, nearly twice its annual average, and the area from New York to Maine and from Ontario to New Brunswick lay under 3 inches (about 8 cm) of ice.

Freezing rain, unlike snow, clings to whatever it hits. Its sheer weight took down millions of trees (including a portion of the area's syrup-producing maple trees), collapsed roofs, and, worst of all, shredded power lines. More than 3 million people across Canada and the northern United States went without electricity for as long as 23 days while crews worked to restore thousands of miles of downed wire. Some grids were so badly damaged they had to be rebuilt almost from scratch. "It looks like a bomb blew up, or someone with a chainsaw came and chopped up everything," a New York State fireman commented.

Meanwhile, residents huddled in the dark without running water, refrigeration, or heat. A cold snap followed

the icefall, and people did what they could to stay warm. Thousands moved to temporary shelter in schools and churches. Parents shut their children in idling cars. Others powered up generators and kerosene heaters, which caused 153 cases of carbon monoxide poisoning in Maine alone. Of the more than 30 deaths related to the storm, only 7 resulted from the initial icefall; most succumbed to hypothermia.

On January 7, the Canadian military deployed its largest force since the Korean War to help with evacuation and cleanup. Three days later, U.S. president Bill Clinton declared 47 northern counties federal disaster areas; they eventually received more than $60 million in aid.

These high-voltage towers south of Montreal, Canada, collapsed under the weight of ice. Nearly 3 million residents in Quebec lost power due to the storm. Below: A tree branch encased in ice. The 1998 ice storm destroyed millions of trees and caused maple syrup production to fall 15 percent in Canada.

EFFECTS ON PLANT LIFE

The 1998 storm varnished most tree branches with a frozen shell up to 3 inches (7.5 cm) thick, which made them 50 to 100 times their normal weight. All told, an average tree supported about two tons of ice. Some handled the strain better than others.

Trees that were bent, rather than broken, stood a better chance of surviving. Old, large trees with heavy limbs fared worse than flexible saplings. Evergreens hid many of their lateral branches below small, cone-shaped crowns, whereas deciduous trees exposed more branches to the ice. Limbs that slope downward tend to incur less damage than horizontal or upright branches.

Ground plants can suffer in freezing rain, too. A long-lasting ice sheet will suffocate bulbs under the soil and chill aboveground species. The longer the ice takes to melt, the worse a plant's chances.

The Blizzard of 1993

A satellite image of the storm complex, taken on March 13, 1993. Residents from the Gulf of Mexico to Canada were affected by the massive storm system.

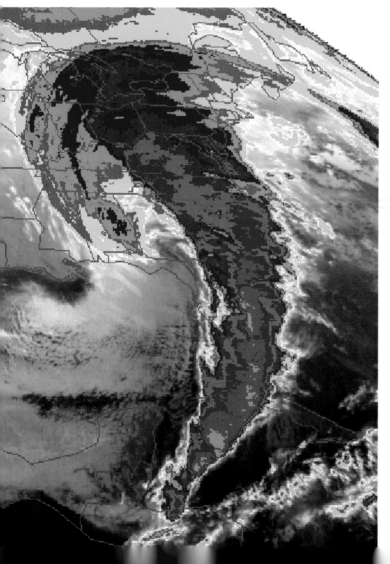

The computers recognized it seemingly before it even existed. Five days before the costliest blizzard in U.S. history slammed into the East Coast, computer models at the National Weather Service detected all the ingredients for a monster storm. Then, early

SPECIFICATIONS

THE BLIZZARD OF 1993
Accumulation: Seven states received more than 40 inches (1 m) of snow
Most snow: 56 inches (1.4 m) in Mount LeConte, Tennessee
Lowest temperature: -12°F (-24°C) in Burlington, Vermont, and Caribou, Maine
Deaths: 200 to 300
Injuries: more than 600
Damages: $2 billion to $6 billion; 3 million customers without power at height of storm
Highest wind speed: gusts of 144 mph (232 km/h) at Mount Washington, New Hampshire

on March 12, 1993, an infant cyclone began to feed on atmospheric instability in the western Gulf of Mexico. By nightfall it had become, according to one meteorologist, "a storm with the heart of a blizzard and the soul of a hurricane." Over the next three days, as the squall seethed northward, it sprayed spasms of weather's worst in every direction: blizzards, tornadoes, torrential rains, storm surges, record cold, and hurricane-speed winds.

Florida was the first victim. As the storm matured, it turned toward Florida's west coast, pushing a cold front that caused 12-foot (4 m) waves that drowned more people than Hurricanes Hugo and Andrew put together, and 11 confirmed tornadoes. Once the storm made landfall, it barreled north, smothering a third of the United States, from

Alabama to Maine, in up to 5 feet (1.5 m) of snow. It had dropped 13 cubic miles (54 cubic km) of snow by the time it dissipated, the equivalent of 56,000 Empire State Buildings.

Atlantic Coast Shuts Down

The storm crushed roofs, knocked out power for some three million people, and caused anywhere from $2 billion to $6 billion in property damage. New York's governor, Mario Cuomo, figured that plowing alone would cost $120 million. The storm also brought the eastern seaboard to an abrupt halt: The interstate highways closed from Atlanta north, and, for the first time, every major airport on the Atlantic Coast shut down, grounding a quarter of the nation's flights. Record low temperatures, including 17 degrees Fahrenheit (-8°C) in Montgomery, Alabama, and -12°F (-24°C) in Burlington, Vermont, kept the snow from melting.

Polar bears are able to survive the Arctic climate due to several physical adaptations. Their thick, white fur allows sunlight to pass through so heat is absorbed by the bear's black skin. A layer of insulating fat underneath the skin keeps warmth from escaping.

LIFE IN FROZEN REGIONS

Sure, New Englanders can handle the occasional blizzard. But what about the plants, animals, and people living in the Arctic, who endure six-month winters that dip to -29°F (-34°C)? How do they survive, even thrive?

Arctic plants have adapted to freezing temperatures in many ways. Some cling close to the dark soil, which radiates heat and warms the surrounding air by as much as 10°F (12°C). Different species may grow together in clumps to shield one another from the wind. Animals keep warm under heavy layers of fur or feathers and fat; some conserve energy by hibernating though the long, dark winters.

Humans have lived in Arctic regions for at least 40,000 years. Traditionally, the native people heat their homes with oil from the fat of their prey and wear clothes and shoes made from animal skin with the fur left on, which provides both insulation and water resistance. A diet of high-fat foods, like whale blubber, supplies the body with enough fuel to warm itself.

Despite the early, accurate forecast, the storm's intensity caught America—particularly the South—by surprise. Many southerners have grown deaf to empty threats from their meteorologists about hurricanes and thunderstorms. "I can remember going to bed the night before and thinking, 'Boy, the Weather Service must be losing it,'" an Alabama radio-station employee remembered. "It was in the low to mid-fifties with rain. The phone rang around five AM and I was called to work. Four days later I returned home."

But few who heeded the warnings in mid-March could have known how to prepare. A winter storm this bad had not hit the South in living memory.

Northern Arkansas had an unusually high accumulation of snowfall during the storm. Most of the southern states were taken by surprise by the storm's severity.

A resident of Westchester County, New York, clears off her car on the day after a foot of snow was dumped on the region by the so-called "storm of the century."

Thousands of people were stranded by record depths of snow. Helicopters airlifted nine hikers out of the Smoky Mountains on March 18, and 190 more were rescued in the surrounding Appalachians.

Given the extent of the storm—more than half the country's population was affected—fixing exact casualty num-bers turned out to be impossible. Most official estimates range from 200 to 300 deaths directly attributable to the storm (not including 48 lost at sea and countless shoveling-induced hearts attacks) and more than 600 injuries. In Florida, flood-ing, tornadoes, and wind-weaponized rubble killed 44 people. Pennsylvania suf-fered the highest mortality, with 49 dead.

DRIVING SAFETY

In a winter storm, the safest route is to stay home. But when you have to get in your car, drive slowly: Speed limits assume ideal conditions. Braking requires twice as much distance or more on ice and snow, so leave extra space between yourself and the vehicle in front of you. Switch your headlights on to make your car more visible to other drivers.

Every action—braking, turning, changing lanes—should be smooth, not jerky or abrupt. To avoid skidding on icy roads, brake gradually. Should your car begin to skid, ease up on the brake and steer in the direction of the skid.

Be particularly careful on bridges and overpasses—they can ice over even when the regular roads stay dry.

Hailstorms: Germany, 1984, and China, 2002

Munich, only 30 miles (48 km) north of the foothills of the Alps, often suffers from violent, unexpected weather. Wind that blows down from the slopes can chill a hot day or heat a cool one within hours, and thunderstorms frequently churn up in the cauldron between the mountains and the Danube River. On average, one in every ten of these storms brings hail.

The morning of July 12, 1984, showed promise of a calm day. The week before, the city had been gripped by a heat wave: Temperatures climbed to 98°F (37°C), about 25 degrees higher than average. But on July 11 a cold front rolled in from France, bringing respite from the heat.

Background: Hailstones on a field after a summer hailstorm.

Below: Ice floating on the Danube River.

SPECIFICATIONS

GERMANY, 1984
Hail impact velocity: 95 mph (153 km/h)
Depth of fallen hail in Munich: 7 inches (18 cm)
Hailstorm's swath: 155 miles (250 km) by
   3 to 9 miles (5–15 km), from Lake
   Constance to near the Austrian border
Injuries: 300 to 400
Insurance claims: cars, EUR 450 million
   (US$ 601 million); buildings and houses,
   EUR 200 million (US$ 267 million);
   miscellaneous, EUR 100 million (US$ 134 million)

The citizens of Munich awoke on July 12 to a cloudless sky. Through late afternoon, there were no signs that the area was hours away from one of the most costly weather events in German history.

Pummeled by Ice

That morning, off to the south, a super-storm was brewing. The cold front that had relieved southern Germany settled under a layer of humid, warm air. Because the cold front was denser, the layers remained fairly stable—that is, until the sun began to heat the cold air and a thunderstorm from Switzerland pulled the pressure down. The warming mass rose and mixed with the air above and, fed by the moisture in the upper layer, formed a giant thundercloud—all contributing to perfect conditions for a hailstorm.

The evening's first hailstones fell in Ravensburg, 100 miles (160 km) south-west of Munich, at about 6 PM, causing only minimal damage. But as the storm moved northeast, it grew more massive and ferocious, sucking moisture from the lakes of Bavaria and forming larger and larger hailstones. Barreling ahead at 40 miles per hour (65 km/h), the storm reached the outskirts of Munich at 8 PM. The temperature suddenly plunged from 80°F (27°C) to 60°F (15°C). For the next 20 minutes, hailstones up to 4 inches (10 cm) in diameter, one of which was reported to weigh 28 ounces (0.79 kg), bombarded the city at 95 miles per hour (153 km/h), shattering windows, crushing roofs, pummeling crops, and flattening cars. By the time the thunderclouds departed for Austria two hours later, Munich lay under a 7-inch (18 cm) coating of ice, which even at the height of summer did not melt until morning.

Luckily, the hail itself had not killed anyone, although a 54-year-old man succumbed to a heart attack when a stone smashed through his window. More than 400 people had been injured, however, either from hail impact, shattering glass, or car accidents. The Munich fire department responded to more than 3,800 calls that night.

Hailstones clogged the city's storm drains and melted amid shards of glass on the seats of cars and buses. Few buildings or vehicles escaped the storm unscathed. As drivers found dented heaps of metal where their cars had been parked and shop owners surveyed ruined storefronts, calls flooded the insurance companies. Insurers eventually paid out 1.5 billion deutschmarks ($1.02 billion); the uninsured damage was probably equally high.

Damaged cars at Munich International Airport after the hail-storm dropped egg-size hailstones onto the city.

Right: Torrential rain was just the beginning of China's weather troubles in 2002. This false-color image shows flooding around the Yangtze River that was caused by frequent, heavy rains.

Background: A thick layer of smog over central China photographed from space on July 11, 2002.

SPECIFICATIONS

CHINA, 2002
Highest wind speeds: 45 mph (72 km/h)
Deaths: 22
Injuries: 200

Henan Province, China, July 2002

From the start of 2002, the environment seemed to have declared war on China. Torrential rains hit the southeast in spring and continued through the summer, choking rivers and setting off floods that killed more than 800 people and left another million homeless. Farther north, Beijing endured an infestation of locusts. Scientists blamed the cruel conditions on air pollution or El Niño; neither option offered much hope that relief would come anytime soon.

Then, as if floods and locusts were not enough, at 6:30 PM on July 19 menacing black clouds unleashed a third plague: missiles of ice. Henan and Guangdong provinces were struck with what natives called the worst hailstorm in 50 years: rain, 45 mile per hour (72 km/h) winds, and egg-size stones up

to 2 inches (5 cm) in diameter. In a half hour the storm had passed, but in its wake it left uprooted trees, downed power lines, and hundreds of human casualties. Twenty-two people died, the majority of them crushed when rickety buildings collapsed under the weight of the hail. Some 200 more were injured by falling ice or wind-borne debris; Henan emergency rooms treated a rash of head wounds.

Without Warning

The next morning, fallen trees still blocked the roads, but authorities managed to restore electricity and running water by the end of the day. The residents of Henan had a more significant grievance, however: They had not been given enough time or information to prepare for the storm. The Henan Province Meteorological Station had issued a severe weather warning only an hour before the clouds filled the sky. The warning did not specify where the storm would strike or that it might bring hail. "We said there would be a thunderstorm. It's difficult to predict hail," said Gu Wanlong, the manager of the meteorological station. Nevertheless, residents jammed a government hotline with complaints. "If the warning had reached the public in time," Gu admitted, "a lot of damage might have been avoided, like deaths, injuries, traffic accidents, and collapsed buildings." He blamed the late, incomplete forecast on the station's antiquated radar system.

Yao Daixian, the deputy mayor of Zhengzhou, Henan's capital and one of the hardest-hit cities, laid responsibility for the deaths on shoddy construction. Four of his constituents had been crushed when a gas station collapsed, and in a neighboring village, four more had died when a factory caved in. Yao called for stricter building codes and disaster preparedness, but his demands came too late to save his countrymen to the north. Just two days after the

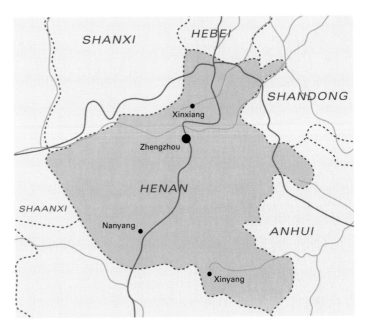

hailstorm in Henan, another hit Ningxia Hui Autonomous Region, hundreds of miles to the northwest, ruining crops, demolishing houses, and causing 50 million renminbi ($6.5 million) in damages.

A map of Henan Province in China. The capital city of Zhengzhou suffered serious damages in the 2002 hailstorm.

RECORD-BREAKING HAIL

The heaviest recorded hail struck in Bangladesh on April 14, 1986, when 92 people were killed by stones weighing as much as 2.2 pounds (1 kg). The largest single hailstone on record was found in Aurora, Nebraska. It measured 18.75 inches (47.62 cm) in circumference. The largest hailstone aggregate by volume measured 20 feet (6 m) long and fell in Ross-shire, Scotland. Scientists postulated that several pieces must have been fused together by lightning. In Yuwu, China, a hailstone aggregate weighed in at 9 pounds (4 kg). Of course, these records do not mean that bigger hail has never fallen. How many massive chunks of ice must have rained down in the millennia before refrigeration could preserve specimens for measurement and authentication? Even today, how many world-record stones fall that no one ever sees or thinks to stick in the freezer?

Avalanches: Peru and Washington State

On the afternoon of May 31, 1970, the people of Yungay, Peru, were enjoying a normal Sunday. Visitors from neighboring villages bustled through the market, while most of the city's 20,000 residents sat glued to radios, listening to the USSR–Mexico match in the 1970 World Cup.

The Fall of Nevado Huascarán

At 3:23 PM, as the scoreless game was winding down, the ground suddenly buckled. An earthquake had torn through northern Peru. In an instant, Yungay was reduced to rubble. Its adobe buildings collapsed; the market was left in splinters. As survivors climbed to their feet, a low roar descended from the mountains. Everyone turned to look. For a few moments, the only clue was a cloud of dust around the northern peak of Nevado Huascarán Mountain. The roar swelled, reaching a deafening scream as the earthquake survivors noticed the first airborne boulders hurtling over the ridge toward them. By 3:28, Yungay was completely submerged under 32 feet (10 m) of ice, mud, and rocks.

Nevado Huascarán in the Peruvian Andes. The mountain's peak rises 22,205 (6,768 m) above sea level.

For the population in the shadow of Peru's highest peak, debris avalanches had become a recurring nightmare. Instead of the tumbling masses of snow most people picture when they think of avalanches, debris avalanches send mud, ice, and rocks racing downhill. In 1962, 13 million tons of debris had barreled down the 22,000-foot (6,700 m) face of Nevado Huascarán's western side, burying nine towns and killing 4,000 people. Yungay, protected by surrounding hills, had survived largely undamaged at that time. The 1962 event was the first major avalanche since pre-Columbian times, but after it occurred, scientists predicted an even bigger one could strike.

The path of the debris avalanche that overran Yungay.

Loss of a Village

The 1970 earthquake—7.7 on the Richter scale—dislodged a chunk of glacial ice and rock 3.5 to 4 miles (5,400 to 6,500 m) up the same face that had unleashed the 1962 slide. As the 3,000-foot-wide (900 m), mile-long mass skidded down the steep slope, it picked up snow, boulders, and mud like a colossal snowball. Both larger and more powerful than the earlier

A large impact crater that measured approximately 8 feet deep, 23 feet wide, and 36 feet long (2.5 x 7 x 11 m) caused by rocks hurled several hundred yards by the avalanche.

avalanche, it spread into areas the previous one had not reached. By the time it swept into Yungay, 10 miles (15 km) from the source at 175 miles per hour (280 km/h), the avalanche was carrying 1,765 to 3,531 million cubic feet (50 to 100 million cu. m) of debris.

Witnesses remember first a blast of air and mud that stripped trees and threw people to the ground. Then, one survivor recalled, "a cresting wave 10

stories high" descended on the village. The seething mass, spitting boulders as far as 2 miles (3.2 km), eventually stretched over 15 miles (25 km), burying several villages and, of course, Yungay. Only 92 people survived in Yungay. The earthquake had killed about 48,000, and the avalanche took more than 18,000 more lives. A month later, the mud over Yungay had baked hard as adobe. Only the walls of the cathedral and a few palm trees poked through to hint at the city buried beneath. Elsewhere, an observer noted,

"many fields were so thoroughly pockmarked with craters that they resembled battlefields."

After 1970 the Peruvian government began fortifying the glacier's natural dam so that it, and the ice behind it, might resist future shocks. Meanwhile, Yungay's survivors rebuilt a few miles north, safely out of the path of whatever falls down Huascarán. The original site remains untouched, officially declared a national cemetery and serving as a monument to the city buried below.

Adobe houses destroyed in Huarez, Peru, during the 1970 earthquake.

Wellington, Washington, 1910

On Friday, February 25, 1910, a blizzard stranded the Great Northern Railway's Spokane local train No. 25 in the Cascade Mountains. Snow blocked the tracks in both directions, and 30 to 40 passengers waited in the rail cars on the slopes of Stevens Pass near Wellington, Washington, while crews dug through the drifts. At first, everyone stayed calm. There was plenty to eat, and the coaches were warm; the workmen would get the train moving soon enough.

But after two days, the plows had burned through the coal supply, food was running low, and the passengers began having premonitions of disaster. "A number of us had heard the timbers cracking with reports like cannon all Sunday evening," one remembered, and on Monday morning the overhanging ledge of snow looked almost ready to tumble. Several men finally decided to hike to safety in the nearby town of Scenic. The others warned them that the trip would be suicide. Instead, they walked away from the worst snow disaster in American history.

Background: The Cascade Mountains in Washington State.

Below: The Washington landscape along the route of the Great Northern Railway in 1914.

SPECIFICATIONS

WASHINGTON, 1910
Size of original slab: 1,320 feet (400 m) wide, 1.5 miles (2.5 km) long
Deaths: 96 (35 passengers and 61 railroad employees)
Survivors: 23
Damages: $1 million, including 2,000 feet (600 m) of track and seven locomotives

Trapped

Small avalanches had already delayed the train twice before it reached Wellington: for 10 hours Tuesday at Leavenworth, Washington, and from Wednesday to Friday at the entrance to the 2.6-mile Cascade Tunnel. Amid snowflakes described as "the size of soda crackers," crews finally cleared the tracks, and the No. 25 was steaming west toward Seattle. It got as far as Wellington, just outside the tunnel's western portal. New snowslides had closed the way both east and west, so the No. 25, followed a few hours later by a mail train, pulled onto a sidetrack near the small town.

On February 28 the blizzard turned into a lightning storm. Thunder jostled the slopes, and rain softened the snow. In the wee hours of March 1, a slab a quarter-mile (400 m) wide and 1.5 miles

"Suddenly there was a dull roar, and the sleeping men and women felt the passenger coaches lifted and borne along."

—AVALANCHE SURVIVOR

(2.5 km) long broke off the snowpack in the hills above Wellington. A railroad employee heard a rumbling and turned to look. "White Death moving down the mountainside above the trains," he recalled. "Relentlessly it advanced, exploding, roaring, rumbling, grinding, snapping—a crescendo of sound that might have been the crashing of 10,000 freight trains. It descended to the ledge where the sidetracks lay, picked up cars and equipment as though they were so many snow-draped toys, and swallowing them up, disappeared like a white, broad monster into the ravine below."

The avalanche swept the two trains and the station 150 feet (45 m) into the ravine. More than a hundred passengers and crew, asleep in the cars when the avalanche hit, lay entombed under 40 feet (12 m) of snow. Rescue crews from neighboring towns, working with shovels and lanterns, dug 23 survivors from the tangle of trees, boulders, and iron, but 96 others died. Three-man teams guided the bodies out on sleds. It took three weeks to clear the tracks of snow and debris before the route could open again.

The Great Northern Railway, now host of the nation's worst rail disaster, quickly began boring a longer tunnel 500 feet (150 m) below the original. Still in use today, the 8-mile (13 km) tunnel allows rail riders to avoid one of the most dangerous sections of track in the United States.

Above: The Great Northern Railway's train number 4 rides along the snow-covered route, c. 1929.

Below: A ski patrolman and his dog perform training exercises in order to gain certification in avalanche rescue.

SURVIVAL AND RESCUE TECHNIQUES

If you ever get caught in an avalanche, chances are you triggered it. Almost all avalanche accidents are caused by the victims themselves. Avalanche safety, therefore, revolves around prevention: teaching skiers, snowmobilers, and climbers—the most common casualties—to recognize dangerous terrain.

Quick rescue is vital and often must be performed by the victim's companions. Victims have a 92 percent chance of surviving if they are rescued within 15 minutes; after 90 minutes, most will have suffocated.

The winter adventurer's most essential equipment is a transceiver that can send a distress signal from under the snow. Companions then use receivers to home in on the victim's location. Otherwise, they will have to probe the snow with poles to find buried victims.

If you get caught in an avalanche, try to swim toward the surface. Scooping out an air pocket before the snow sets will buy crucial time. Most important, remain calm. Steady breathing will prolong your air supply.

CHAPTER 4

FLOODS AND THEIR CONSEQUENCES

IN A MODEL OF THE SOLAR SYSTEM, our planet jumps right out—three-quarters of it is bright blue. Water is essential for life, which is why humans have always inhabited lands near lakes and rivers. But every body of water is capable of breaking its bounds. Among natural disasters, floods are both the most ubiquitous and the most deadly. Humans need water to survive, but too much in the wrong place will crush homes, smother farms, and drown inhabitants.

Whether a hurricane, monsoon, or shifting ocean current is the catalyst, all waterways eventually overflow. Many cultures have stories about cataclysmic floods—from the Babylonian god Enlil's punishment for the noisy humans who kept him awake, to the Lithuanian god Pramzinas who ate nuts while the world drowned, to Noah's 40 days and 40 nights. Yet people still cling to the floodplains because, for all their punishment, deluges also bring rewards. From Mesopotamia and ancient Egypt to modern times, farmers have relied on the rich alluvial soil that is deposited and renewed by unruly rivers.

Left: A composite picture of Earth's Eastern Hemisphere, fusing satellite images taken over several months. From this distance—more than 435 miles (700 km) away—the high ratio of water to land on our planet's surface is obvious; closer to home, our dependence on water for life, transportation, and irrigation comes into focus, evident from the homes that crowd shore-lines and riverbanks. When these waterways overflow, the effects can be both beneficial and deadly. Inset: Girls wade home through floodwaters in the Comilla district of Bangladesh, east of Dhaka, on July 17, 1999. Rising rivers overran the embankments to flood 41 of the nation's 64 districts that summer.

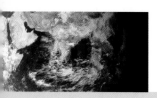

THE GIFT OF THE NILE

For thousands of years, farmers in Egypt have depended on the flooding of the Nile. Every year the river would overrun its banks, spreading a thin layer of rich, alluvial mud along either side. That narrow strip—just 3 percent of Egypt's area—is virtually the country's only farmland, but the mud was so bountiful the planters never needed fertilizer.

Of course the floods—which the Egyptians called the "gift of the Nile"—could be destructive. Recent research has unearthed evidence that the river washed two ancient cities into the sea.

As the population boomed in the twentieth century, Egyptian leaders searched for a way to produce more food. The Aswan dam, which is 11,800 feet (3,600 m) long, was completed in 1970, creating a reservoir that allows farmers to plant all year. But without the annual flooding, farmers now need artificial fertilizer, and the land, no longer strengthened by yearly silt deposits, is vulnerable to erosion.

Above: Sailboats ply the waters of the Nile River near Aswan, in southern Egypt. The periodic flooding of the world's longest river created a fertile sliver along its banks, but it also occasionally washed cities away. Since the completion of the Aswan dam in 1970, dangerous flooding has all but ceased; without annual silt deposits, though, the soil has lost some of its fertility.

Right: The 1889 flood in Johnstown, Pennsylvania, is one of the most devastating on record. This illustration of the Pennsylvania Railroad bridge washing away appeared in an 1889 edition of *Harper's Weekly* magazine. The disaster, in which over 2,200 people were killed, and the subsequent relief and rebuilding effort captivated the American public.

To live with the water is to fear its fury. And although a flood's onslaught can be abrupt, even totally unexpected, the buildup—days or weeks of rain, swelling seas, steadily rising current—happens in slow motion. That unhurried pace, coupled with the foreknowledge of where calamity can strike, makes floods the one kind of natural

disaster that can be prevented. And so people have built dams, dikes, levees, reservoirs, and canals, erecting and bolstering these defenses, with steadily advancing sophistication, for millennia.

Yet these attempts to control nature sometimes result in concentrating its deadly force and can unintentionally deprive plants and animals that depend on floodwaters. And often the rivers, lakes, and oceans expose our levees and dams for what they are—hubris. Few things are as powerful a reminder of the force of nature as several million tons of rushing water.

The Theodore Roosevelt Dam on the Salt River in Arizona, once the tallest masonry dam in the world.

Bangladesh, August 1998 and July 1999

Most of Bangladesh is essentially a single, flat delta. The tiny nation is crisscrossed by 230 rivers, and four—the Ganges (locally called the Padma), Brahmaputra, Jamuna, and Meghna—funnel in huge amounts of water from melting Himalayan snow. The summer monsoons flood as much as a third of Bangladesh every year, but they usually bring good fortune. The floodplains boast some of the country's most fertile, populated land.

The summer of 1998 brought Bangladesh intense monsoon rains, but nothing to suggest the disaster that was about to strike. Furious downpours upriver, in India, coupled with heavy mountain snowmelt, glutted all the major rivers. Then, unusually high tides in the Bay of Bengal blocked the overflow from draining. The Ganges River rose to its highest-ever recorded level, and by the end of August more than two-thirds of the country lay submerged under chest-deep water.

As incredible as the height of the rising water was, it was the duration rather than the depth of the flood that brought the most devastation. The flood lasted over two months—three times longer than any other in the country's history. More than 22 million people were stranded or left home-less. Villagers spent night after night

SPECIFICATIONS

BANGLADESH FLOOD, 1998
Deaths: more than 1,500
Number made homeless: 3 million
Damages: $2 billion
Houses destroyed: 353,000
Cropland destroyed: 2 million acres
  (8,000 sq km)

on the roofs of their shacks; the less fortunate suspended sheets of plastic over wooden platforms. Parents slept in shifts to watch over their children, making sure they were not taken by the brown current. Bridges and thousands of miles of roads were washed out, as were the landfills. People were forced to empty their garbage and sewage into the floodwaters, creating a perfect breeding ground for disease.

By the time the water finally receded in October, more than 1,500 people were dead, many by drowning, some when cobras bit victims in flooded homes, and a huge number from diarrhea. Millions more went hungry. Floodwaters soaked more than 2 million acres (8,000 sq. km) of cropland, destroying 2 million tons of rice. But delivering aid to the stranded population was difficult. Because the strong current in the floodwater washed packages away, supplies could not be airdropped, so boats ferried food to refugees until trucks could pass.

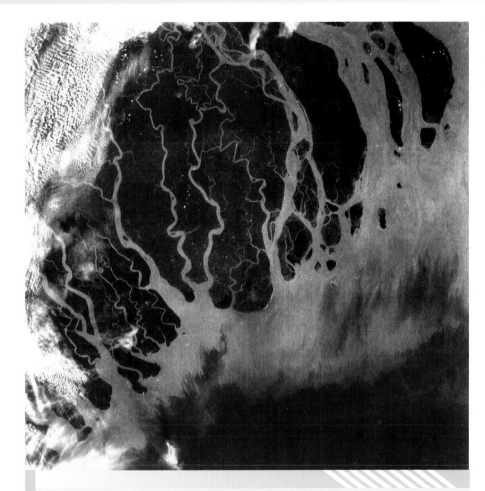

The Ganges Delta from space. One of the longest of the 230 rivers that flow through Bangladesh, the Ganges submerged more than two-thirds of the nation in 1998.

EROSION

Every year erosion kills crops and displaces thousands of Bangladeshis. Trees slow currents and absorb water, but as Southeast Asia's population rises, farmers clear more forests for agriculture. Repeated tilling makes the soil vulnerable to runoff. When rising sea levels or heavy rains strengthen the already mighty Ganges, Jamuna, and Brahmaputra rivers, the force of the current dissolves natural barriers and scours villages and farms. On average, 1,500 miles (2,400 km) of riverbank are ground away annually in Bangladesh. Officials blame erosion for much of the country's poverty.

To combat the problem, engineers have worked to shore up embankments with sand and stone, but the best bet may be learning to use the land in a way that prevents erosion in the first place. A Bangladeshi pineapple farmer, for example, increased his yield by 50 percent simply by planting his hillside crop in horizontal, rather than vertical, rows.

With $1.3 billion in international aid, the country's farmers, fishermen, and laborers had just begun to put their lives back together the following spring when early monsoons swelled the waterways again. Rising rivers burst through man-made barriers in July; the Gomti River crushed a 10-foot (3 m) embankment, mowing down homes and farmland with absolutely no warning. By the end of summer, floodwaters had swamped 41 of Bangladesh's 64 districts, displaced at least 2 million people, damaged 1 million acres (4,000 sq. km) of crops, and killed 19 people.

In response to these back-to-back disasters, Bangladesh shored up its levees, drainage channels, and dams and updated or opened 85 flood-monitoring stations to provide citizens with early warnings.

A Bangladeshi boy boats to school in the Manikgonj district, north of Dhaka, in July 1999. The country had just begun to recover from the 1998 flood when the rivers overflowed once again.

SPECIFICATIONS

BANGLADESH FLOOD, 1999
Deaths: 19 confirmed
Number made homeless: at least 2 million
Houses damaged: 126,000
Cropland damaged: 1 million acres
  (4,000 sq km)

But the fact remains that one of the most flood-prone nations in the world is also one of the most destitute and densely populated—with 125 million citizens in an area of 52,000 square miles (134,000 sq. km). Politics has interfered with international aid and investment efforts in the past, and until the economy can weather another flood, no amount of warning will be enough for the people of Bangladesh.

Flood victims in Narayangonj, Bangladesh, line up for aid on August 26, 1998. Floods in the Ganges Delta destroyed some 1.65 million acres (6,689 sq. km) of crops, which meant that many of the country's 3 million homeless went hungry.

AFTERMATH: HUNGER AND DISEASE

Eighty percent of Bangladeshis earn their living from the land. And when, as happened in 1998, a single flood cuts rice production by 75 percent, a country where starvation lurks even in good years can collapse into famine. The government of Bangladesh at first shied away from asking for outside help, but by August necessity outweighed propriety. Gifts of 1.6 million tons of grain forestalled major famine. When floods struck again the next summer, aid groups were ready. The Red Crescent Society distributed rice to 10,000 families soon after the floods hit.

Disease makes a more elusive foe. Sewage and trash blackened the floodwaters, but villagers still bathed and washed dishes in it; they even drank it. Relief workers struggled to disperse water-purification tablets in a nation with few open roads. More than a million people in the 1998 floods suffered from diarrhea. When the torrent receded, it left behind a dark sludge. Mosquitoes bred in the stagnant water in Dakar—a surefire recipe for malaria.

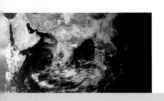

The Mighty Mississippi

Mark Twain wrote of the Mississippi in 1883:

Ten thousand River Commissions, with the mines of the world at their back, cannot tame that lawless stream, cannot curb it or confine it, cannot say to it, Go here, or Go there, and make it obey; cannot save a shore which it has sentenced; cannot bar its path with an obstruction which it will not tear down, dance over, and laugh at.

The next hundred years would prove Twain wrong, as Americans learned how to make the river obey. But eventually, to the great cost of the inhabitants, his wisdom was confirmed.

A member of the Spanish explorer Hernando de Soto's expedition to the New World in 1539 noted that when the rains hit, the Native Americans along the Mississippi retreated behind piled-up heaps of earth. These crude dirt mounds were the opening act in an escalating saga to tame America's longest, most vital, most recalcitrant waterway. Since the early 1700s, when European settlers put up the first levees, the Mississippi has become one of the most engineered rivers in the world.

In the mid-1800s the Army Corps of Engineers began to build high levees along both banks. They reasoned that, deprived of floods, the sheer force of

Right: A map of the Mississippi River, which runs from the state of Minnesota to the Gulf of Mexico. The lower section, beginning in Illinois, is lined with 1,700 miles (2,700 km) of levees, the latest manifestation of a centuries-long effort to control its flooding.

SPECIFICATIONS

THE 1927 FLOOD
Area of flood: 27,000 square miles (70,000 sq km)
Deaths: 246
Displaced: 700,000
Damages: $347 million in 1927 dollars (about $4 billion in 2006 dollars)
Buildings destroyed: 2,200

MINNESOTA

WISCONSIN

IOWA

ILLINOIS

MISSOURI

KENTUCKY

TENNESSEE

ARKANSAS

LOUISIANA

MISSISSIPPI

"I saw a whole tree just disappear, sucked under by the current, then saw it shoot up, it must have been a hundred yards [downstream]. Looked like a missile fired by a submarine."

—A WITNESS TO THE 1926 STORM

the current would engrave a deeper channel, which would not only prevent future overflows, but also facilitate navigation. Beginning in 1878 and continuing into the twentieth century, the corps erected dams and dikes to narrow the river. The lower Mississippi—from Cairo, Illinois, to the Gulf—is now walled by about 1,700 miles (2,700 km) of levees.

But the river rebelled. Confined, the water level jumped even faster, and the Army Corps jacked up the embankments to match: Levees that had started out at 7 feet (2 m) grew to 38 feet (12 m) by 1927. The bulging current presented only the first in a series of unintended consequences of interference with the Mississippi.

Engineering has also altered the surrounding landscape. Wetlands, including much of the ecosystem in Louisiana and Mississippi, depend on flooding for moisture and deposits of fertile silt. By containing floods, levees on the lower Mississippi have helped shrink the active floodplain by 90 percent. Without replenishment of flood sediment, Louisiana's marshes have shriveled by more than 1,500 square miles (3,900 sq. km) in the past 70 years.

Scientists hypothesize that if the river were freed from its constraints, the wetlands' problems would disappear. Left alone, a river constantly changes course: One channel silts up, and the current creates another during the next flood. Without its dams and levees, the Mississippi might have shifted to the Atchafalaya River as its primary outlet to the Gulf, as it has done periodically in the past, rather than continue its present path through Baton Rouge and New Orleans.

Marshes in the Mississippi Delta. Louisiana's marshes have shrunk by more than 1,500 square miles (3,885 sq. km) since the 1927 flood, due in part to levees and embankments that prevent the Mississippi River from flooding.

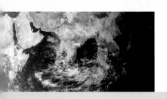

In fact, a panel of scientists and engineers in April 2006 recommended just that: Let the river shift. As it is now, the delta flushes silt deep into the Gulf. A new channel might release sediments where tides, currents, and waves would return them to shore—spreading as much as a half-inch over 60 square miles (155 sq. km) per year. In an era of rising oceans, that's plenty to officials in Louisiana, where the land drops as far as 8 feet (2.4 m) below sea level.

The 1927 Flood

Ask an old-timer on the Delta what he fears, and he will reply, "God and the Mississippi." The river pays and punishes with equal, gigantic force. The stretch between Memphis and New Orleans is some of the most fertile land in America. Generations of cotton planters made their fortunes there. But when the mile-wide, hundred-foot-deep river runs out of control, massive destruction results.

Native Americans warned European explorers that the river would flood every 14 years. But rather than adapt to its moods, white settlers vowed to control it. Early farmers built their own, usually ineffective, embankments to restrain floodwaters. Then, in 1850, the Army Corps of Engineers lined both banks from Cairo, Illinois, to New Orleans with levees that eventually loomed four stories high. The engineers were so confident they had conquered nature that they rejected all supplemental measures, such as reservoirs and runoff outlets. In 1926 the corps announced that its levees had forever tamed the Mississippi. But the truth was that by restricting the river, the levees were actually raising the water levels.

The Rising River

In the fall of 1926, storms across the North fed the Mississippi. The next spring, rainfall reached 10 times the annual average. Huge swells started surging down the river. In February tributaries rammed through levees in Arkansas, dousing more than 100,000 acres (400 sq. km) with 10 to 15 feet (3–4.5 m) of water. On April 15, 15 inches (38 cm) of rain fell on the Delta in 18 hours, and the river began to rise as much as 2 feet (0.6 m) per day. The first of the government levees to burst was in Illinois on April 16. More than 2 million acres (8,000 sq. km) were submerged.

A dog survives the flood by climbing onto the roof of a Murphy, Mississippi, home. The flood destroyed approximately 2,200 buildings.

Downriver, the residents of Mississippi and Louisiana had been growing more frightened by the moment, especially when the Mounds Landing levee, 12 miles (19 km) north of Greenville, Mississippi, started to weaken.

The Response

When society responds to disaster, social divisions often come into focus. On the Delta in the 1920s, African Americans were treated much as they had been during slavery. Many blacks had left the South during the preceding decades, but the plantations in the Mississippi Delta region still relied on their cheap labor. As the white population fled, police began rounding up African Americans at gunpoint to fix the embankments. Some 30,000 African Americans piled sandbags on top of the Mounds Landing embankment. However, the levees would not hold for long.

The Levee Fails

On the morning of April 21, rivulets of water started poking through the base of the levee. "It was just boiling up," one worker said. "The levee just started shaking. You could feel it shaking." When the water began to dislodge the sandbags, the workers ignored the guns and ran. Finally, the river blasted open a gash three-quarters of a mile (1.2 km) wide that unleashed a 100-foot-high wall of water that washed away many of the workers.

Around Mounds Landing, the Delta was now an ocean. Surges from the broken dam rushed 60 miles (95 km) east and 90 miles (145 km) south, and floodwater spread over 27,000 square miles (70,000 sq. km), the area of Massachusetts, Connecticut, New Hampshire, and Vermont combined. Downriver, officials dynamited the Poydras levee to divert the deluge from

Above: After a season of savage rains, flood-waters gush though the breach in the Mounds Landing levee near Greenville, Mississippi, in April 1927. Although police had forced the region's blacks at gunpoint to bolster the embankment, it collapsed April 21, flooding more than 27,000 square miles (70,000 sq. km).

Below: Water and wreckage litter downtown Valmeyer, Illinois, on October 10, 1993. After the 1993 flood, the residents of Valmeyer rebuilt their entire town on higher ground a little over a mile to the east of the original site.

NORTH DAKOTA, 1993

The 1993 flood of the Mississippi, which submerged 16,000 square miles (41,400 sq. km) in nine states, devoured several midwestern towns whole. The deluge destroyed 50,000 homes and inflicted $15 billion to $20 billion in damages. Afterward, officials debated fortifying private levees and increasing the absorbency of the soil. FEMA, on the other hand, decided the best way to reduce damages and deaths was to get homeowners out of the river's way.

In 1994 FEMA began buying flooded property to encourage residents to move somewhere safer. The residents of Valmeyer, Illinois, rebuilt their entire town a mile and a half (2.5 km) east of the original site. By 1997 FEMA had purchased more than 2,000 properties in Illinois.

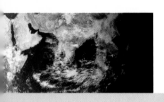

New Orleans, which lay 12 miles (19 km) to the north; they hoped that by removing a barrier to the Gulf, they might allow the river to empty fast enough to spare the city. Elsewhere, the flood topped roofs 75 miles (120 km) from the Mounds Landing breach. The sheer force of the outpouring water steamrolled trees and buildings, while panicked survivors clung to trees and rooftops. One resident remembered, "When it got light enough for us to see, you could see horses, cows, and dogs, and everything else, right in that water, drowning. I thought we was all going to drown."

More than 200 people did drown before rescue arrived. Crews drafted every rowboat and skiff they could find; Arkansas bootleggers, with their fast motorboats, rushed down to help. The flood obliterated 2,200 buildings and damaged 100,000 more, leaving almost a million people homeless. Since sanitation facilities had been wiped out, refugees who remained in the area risked cholera and typhoid. Still, the cotton planters in Greenville feared that if they allowed blacks to evacuate, they would never return. So, 13,000 black workers were sequestered in a tent city patrolled by the National Guard and forced to repair the levee. "All negroes in Greenville outside of the levee camp who are able to work should work," read an order from the chairman of the Washington County Relief Committee. "If work is offered them and they refuse to work they should be arrested as vagrants. Names and addresses of those refusing to work should be telephoned to police headquarters. I suggest one dollar a day as a fair wage at this time."

Federal Relief?
The day after the levee collapsed, President Calvin Coolidge chose Herbert Hoover, the secretary of commerce and a 1928 presidential hopeful, to lead the relief effort. Hoover arrived in Greenville April 26 and approved the plan to make blacks fix the levee. In the past Washington had left disaster relief to local governments, and Coolidge, an advocate of small government, long resisted public pressure to provide

A car tries to make its way down a waterlogged Blanche Avenue in Mounds, Illinois, March 29, 1927. The Mississippi topped 52 feet (15.8 m) in nearby Cairo. (Note that this is far from Mounds Landing, the site of the levee breach, which is in the state of Mississippi.)

more federal support for the devastated Delta. Finally, in May 1928, after a year of public outcry, he allowed federal aid to the flooded areas; until then, the area's largest benefactor was the American Red Cross.

But even that organization's food, clothing, and inoculations went to whites first; only blacks who worked on the levee could expect any rations. Rumors of rapes and assaults by National Guardsmen in the labor

camps filtered to the northern press. Hoover formed a commission of powerful black conservatives to investigate the charges, but he later persuaded them to withhold their findings in exchange for his potential presidential support for social reform. He won the 1928 election, of course, but the promised reforms were not forthcoming. The commission members in turn urged blacks to vote for Franklin D. Roosevelt in 1932.

The flood finally began to ebb in June, and as the waters vanished, so did the Mississippi's sharecroppers. After 200 years of slavery and another 50 of Jim Crow laws, blacks considered their mistreatment during the flood the last straw. A year later, half the Delta's blacks had moved north.

Above: Herbert Hoover, left, and Charles Curtis, right, were inaugurated as president and vice president of the United States on March 4, 1929. Two years earlier, as secretary of commerce, Hoover had coordinated the relief operation in the Mississippi flood region. When, as president, Hoover broke the promises for social reform he had made after the flood, he lost the support of many prominent African Americans.

Left: African Americans in a tent village in Vicksburg Military Park in Vicksburg, Mississippi. While many of the area's whites were rescued and transported out of the region, black refugees were forced to perform repair work.

Bottom: An abandoned car is overwhelmed by floodwaters on a suburban street. Cars can float in just 2 feet (0.6 m) of water, so if the road ahead looks washed out, drivers should turn around.

FLASH FLOODS

Flash floods rise rapidly, are often localized, and are frequently very destructive. In the United States these floods claim more lives than any other weather disaster. The catastrophic failures of dams or levees sometimes cause flash floods, but more often they are the result of deluges caused by long, intense thunderstorms on already saturated ground. An overwhelmed river or stream spills water over its banks, and buildings and pavement inhibit the land's ability to absorb moisture. Within a matter of minutes, a wall of water frothing with rocks and debris can be generated, which knocks down anything in its way. Nearly half the people killed in flash floods die in their cars. A vehicle can float in just two feet of water (0.6 m), and a fast-moving current can throw even an SUV off a bridge.

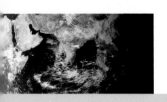

Yangtze River, China, 1931

The nineteenth-century Chinese emperor Tao Kuang nicknamed the Yellow River "China's sorrow." The silt-choked, 2,878-mile (4,632 km) waterway has flooded 1,500 times over the last 3,500 years, killing more people than any other natural feature on Earth. By contrast, China's longest river, the Yangtze, which runs roughly parallel some 420 miles (680 km) to the south, lets loose a major flood maybe once or twice a decade. But the years of quiet belie a ferocious heart. The 3,900-mile (6,200 km) Yangtze spews 5.76 million gallons (22,000 cu. m) of water into the East China Sea on a normal day, which is 18 times as much as the Yellow River does.

China's terrain slopes like a temple roof. The altitude drops 4.5 vertical miles (7.2 km) between the western mountains and the flat, muddy east. All the moisture in the west, from mountain snowmelt to summer rain, rolls across central China like a ball down a hill. Unfortunately, the monsoons hit in late spring, just as the snow is beginning to melt. This combination pours bloated torrents down the Yellow and the Yangtze, China's two longest rivers. A little extra rain or a warmer-than-usual spring is apt to set off a catastrophe—and unfortunately this occurs with dismal regularity.

History of Inundation

Flood stories weave throughout Chinese history. Settled 500,000 years ago, China's central plains are made fertile by rich silt deposits, which are renewed by frequent inundations. Chinese archives hold dike plans dating back 2,000 years; the tales of legendary floods—and venerated river tamers—go back even further. Tradition holds that in 2300 BCE, a Yellow River flood persisted for 13 years. The people blamed their ruler for the river's bad behavior, so the emperor assigned an engineer named Yu to prevent future outbursts. With all the regime's money and manpower at his disposal, Yu dredged a deeper channel and dug diversion outlets—and held the Yellow in check for 1,600 years. The Chinese have a saying: "We should have been fish, but for Yu."

The floods did eventually return, of course. Some priests tried to appease the river with ritual human sacrifice, until a magistrate outlawed the practice in about 400 BCE. But most communities put their faith in ever more extensive and advanced dikes. Levee construction came under government control during the Han dynasty (202 BCE–220 CE); after that, success in flood-control tended to coincide with times the emperor was untroubled by war or insurrection.

"At first we noticed only the obviously flooded fields along the banks of the river, . . . Then gradually we became aware of a number of 'lakes' which constantly increased until finally they gave the impression of one big lake."

—ANNE MORROW LINDBERGH, WIFE OF CHARLES LINDBERGH, ON THEIR AERIAL SURVEYS OF THE FLOOD ZONE

SPECIFICATIONS

CHINA, 1931
Area affected: 70,000 square miles
   (180,000 sq km)
Drowned: 140,000 people
Total killed, including by famine and disease:
   3.7 million
Homeless: 40 million; 40 percent of the
   population in the flood zone had to
   move for the winter
Damages: $1.4 billion (1931 US$)

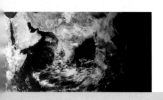

Background: The Yellow River in Lanzhou, China. This river's frequent floods have earned it the nickname China's sorrow, but it was the powerful Yangtze, the nation's longest river, that flooded 70,000 square miles (180,000 sq. km) and drowned 140,000 people in 1931.

As the years progressed, the dike designs grew more sophisticated, but until the mid-twentieth century the engineers' tools remained the Chinese peasantry and the plants and stones at their feet. Millions of peasants worked on the dikes over the centuries, piling up multistory embankments, bundling tiers of rocks with willow branches, and hauling earth in wheelbarrows. Their efforts have no doubt saved countless lives, but they could not possibly prevent disaster forever.

Twentieth-Century Disaster

The monsoon season in 1931 was particularly vicious: In July, seven cyclonic storms raged across the Yangtze basin one after another. Not only did they engorge the Yangtze; they also congested its more than 700 tributaries. When the smaller rivers emptied into the already swollen Yangtze, they created six flood waves that ripped down the river for days. The river ballooned 97 feet (30 m) higher than normal in mid-August, shattering 23 dams and 1,000 levees and submerging 70,000 square miles (180,000 sq. km) of some of the world's most populous, fertile land— an area equal to the states of New York, New Jersey, and Connecticut combined. More than 140,000 people drowned in the first days, many as

they slept. Entire villages were flushed away in the muddy current, and the residents of others floated 20 feet (6 m) above the ground on rafts improvised from doors or bathtubs, waiting for relief.

International Involvement

At the time of the flood, China's Nationalist government had been embroiled in a civil war with the Communists for five years. In the meantime the country's breadbasket, an area that by the 1980s produced a large percentage of the world's rice and grain, was underwater. Not only did refugees lack shelter from the hot summer sun as temperatures reached 100°F (38°C) in the port city of Hankow in August, but they had nothing to eat. The government quickly produced $600,000 in aid, to which the American Red Cross added $100,000, the pope $13,000, and Emperor Hirohito of Japan $27,000. Hirohito's donation was made just weeks before his country invaded China.

The League of Nations offered the use of its epidemiologists, and the U.S. Navy ran communications between Hankow and Shanghai, since China's telegraphs were down. America's famous aviator, Charles Lindbergh, arrived to survey the

flooded areas and help distribute food and medicine. During one drop, starving Chinese peasants tore open a box of medical supplies, hoping for food. "It was one of the most heartrending, yet terrifying scenes I ever saw," Lindbergh said. In the end, relief workers helped 3 million people in 269 counties, distributed 500,000 articles of clothing, and treated 2.5 million sick or injured. One million homeless moved into relief camps.

Meanwhile the flood continued to take lives. By the time the waters receded six months later, more than 3.7 million people had died, most

from famine, others from cholera or dysentery spread by the filthy water.

After 1931 China's national flood relief commission worked 20 years to dig a new retention basin and build enough dikes and levees to, according to the government, "encircle the Earth at its equator."

The Three Gorges Project, which includes the 600-foot-high (180 m) Three Gorges Dam, will create a 400-square-mile (1,000 sq. km) reservoir for Yangtze overflow. Unfortunately, this effort to protect China from the floods will displace millions of residents, destroying their villages.

Construction of the Xiaolangdi Dam on the Yellow River. Completed in 2000, the dam cost $3.5 billion to build and required the resettlement of 200,000 people.

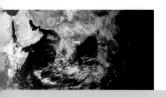

The Johnstown Flood of 1889

Andrew Carnegie. The steel magnate was a member of the South Fork Fishing & Hunting Club, the organization responsible for maintaining the South Fork Dam. Although the club was never found liable for damages and none of the members ever publicly expressed remorse, Carnegie rebuilt Johnstown's library and donated $10,000 to the relief effort.

The morning of May 31, 1889, water ran in the streets of Johnstown, Pennsylvania. For the little steel town in an Allegheny valley, flooding was an annual nuisance. Johnstown sat in the fork of two rivers, the Stonycreek and the Little Conemaugh, which flowed down from the mountains and met to form the Conemaugh River at the town's western edge. Every spring, at least one of the rivers overflowed into Johnstown's increasingly posh parlors. So after a heavy rainstorm on May 30, townspeople began to drag their valuables into the attic as a matter of habit.

The Reverend Dr. David Beale thought his family members were over-reacting. "I had been in my study, on the first floor, preparing for the Sabbath services, when, contrary to my own judgment of the necessity of the case, I was induced to go into my parlor to assist in taking up the carpet. In a moment after I heard a sound as of an approaching railroad train, when all at once the mighty torrent struck our residence. I cried 'Upstairs! Upstairs!'" he later wrote. "The water was on the second story sooner than I was, and carried the hat rack with such force as to strike me on the back, just as I reached the head of the stairs, up to my waist in water."

South Fork Dam Break

He, and the rest of town, immediately realized what must have happened: The South Fork Dam had burst. The dam had been built 14 miles (22 km) up the Little Conemaugh in 1852 to create a canal reservoir. But after the Pennsylvania Railroad made the canal system obsolete, the South Fork Fishing & Hunting Club bought the reservoir to use as a pleasure lake. The club, made up of 61 Pittsburgh industrialists including Andrew Carnegie and Henry Clay Frick, built cabins and stocked the lake with bass, but they failed to maintain the dam.

On the morning of May 31, after the worst rainstorm ever recorded in the area, the club's president noticed that the water in the lake was rising 4 to 6 inches (10 to 15 cm) each hour. He and a group of laborers frantically dug a spillway and raised the height of the dam, but by 2:30 PM water started pouring over the top. By 3:15, the whole structure crumbled and sent 20 million tons of water rushing down the valley at 40 miles per hour (65 km/h).

The 40-foot-high (12 m) wall of water barreled into Johnstown at 4:07 with a thunderous roar, bristling with

"I could see a huge wall advancing with incredible rapidity down the diagonal street. It was not recognizable as water, it was a dark mass in which seethed houses, freight cars, trees, and animals."

—SURVIVOR VICTOR HEISER, WHO WAS **16** AT THE TIME OF THE FLOOD

railroad cars and chunks of buildings. It bulldozed houses, drowning some people in an instant, while others scrambled to stay afloat on buoyant roofs and lumber.

"Our building was raised aloft and whirled away by mad, rushing, bounding and boiling waters of the Little Conemaugh," one survivor remembered. "Eight men were on this roof, and all around us were screaming hundreds of men, women and children. Many of them were swept into eternity; some were praying, some weeping and wailing and some cursing."

"I could see the fearful flood crunching and crackling the houses in its fearful grasp, with no possibility of escape,"

recalled Henry Viering, a furniture dealer. "In a flash I saw my three dear children licked up by it and disappear from sight, as I and my wife were thrown in the air by the rushing ruins. I recovered instantly, in time to see my wife's head just disappearing under water.

"Like lightning I grasped her by the hair, and as best I could, pinioned as I was above the water by the timber, I raised her above it. The weight proved too much, and she sank again. Again I pulled her to the surface, and again she sank. This I did again and again without avail. She drowned in that grasp, and at last dropped from my nerveless hands, to leave my sight forever!"

Johnstown after the flood. In addition to the property damage, one in ten residents of the town was killed in the flood, and 25,000 were made homeless. Survivors huddled in tents or Red Cross shelters and began the work of rebuilding.

Media Frenzy and Aftermath

Viering's experience was, unfortunately, tragically common that day. One in ten citizens of Johnstown died May 31—over 2,200 people in total, including 99 entire families. Bodies were washed as far as Cincinnati, 600 miles (970 km) away. The flood destroyed 4 square miles (10 sq. km) of downtown Johnstown—including 1,600 homes—and left 25,000 refugees.

Their plight made the headlines of newspapers around the country the next day; 100 reporters flocked to Johnstown to cover the story. It was the media sensation of the era. The first book on the flood came out exactly a week after the event, followed by postcards, poetry, commemorative spoons, even a mechanical recreation at Coney Island. The press attention inspired readers to donate $3,742,818.78 to help the residents of Johnstown.

In its first major peacetime effort, the American Red Cross arrived just five days after the flood. Led by Clara Barton, the group distributed food, medicine, and clothing and set up shelters.

In the days following the flood, survivors pitched tents among the mud and debris on the sites of their former homes. The steel mills opened the next week, and in a month stores on Main Street were back in business. By 1910 Johnstown's population had doubled.

Finding Fault

After the South Fork Hunting & Fishing Club turned the reservoir on the Little Conemaugh and 160 acres around it into a resort, they kept up only the most cursory maintenance of the dam while at the same time making dire modifications. They installed screens to prevent their 1,000 black bass from escaping through the spillways. The screens clogged with debris, blocking a crucial overflow drain. To allow two carriages to pass at once, the club also lowered the top of the dam until it rose only 4 feet (1 m) above the spillway. Residents of Johnstown worried at first that the dam would fail, but after 10 uneventful years, the fears became more of a local joke than a serious concern.

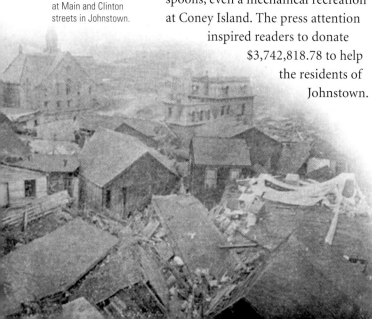

Roofs and piles of debris mark where houses had once stood at Main and Clinton streets in Johnstown.

But after the Johnstown flood and its widespread coverage in the media, in perhaps the first backlash against the powerful, wealthy, sometimes unscrupulous postbellum industrial giants, Americans denounced the South Fork Club. "Manslaughter or Murder?" asked a *Chicago Herald* headline. "We think we know what struck us, and it was not the work of Providence," the *Chicago Tribune* stated in its first edition after the flood. "Our misery is the work of man." The *New York World* was more direct: A June 7 headline read, "The Club is Guilty."

In 1889, though, a judge ruled the flood an "act of God," not of man. None of the club members were ever found liable for the failure of the dam. Although none of them ever publicly expressed remorse, whether they harbored guilty consciences is another question. Half of the members donated to the relief effort. Andrew Carnegie alone gave $10,000, in addition to rebuilding Johnstown's library.

Survivors marvel at the scene in Johnstown, Pennsylvania, after the May 1889 flood. Some 1,600 homes and $17 million in property were destroyed, including 4 square miles (10 sq. km) of downtown Johnstown.

FLOOD WARNING SIGNS

A hurricane or tropical storm is an obvious threat. Other warning signs that your area might flood include hard rain over several hours or days, perhaps coinciding with the spring thaw. Rising water in streams provides early warning, and flooding will most likely hit low-lying areas first. If you see water rising on roads or bridges, turn around and seek higher ground. When in doubt, listen for reports from your local weather service. A flood watch means the weather event is likely; a flood warning means the event is about to occur or is already occurring.

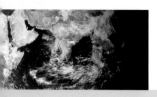

Guatemalan Mudslide

In the United States the most active Atlantic hurricane season on record will be remembered for one name: Katrina. But in a year with 15 hurricanes, four of them category 5, it was a relatively small, category 1 storm that left its mark in Central America. Hurricane Stan struck late in the season and never mustered the wind speeds of Rita or Wilma, but it topped the death tolls of both these hurricanes.

Hurricane Stan hit Mexico's Gulf Coast on October 4, 2005, dumping rain from Veracruz to Costa Rica before weakening to a tropical depression that night. As dawn broke on October 5, storms spawned by Stan continued to dump rain on the region. Rivers overflowed in Mexico and Guatemala, rain washed out bridges, and wind-downed trees blocked roads, but the worst seemed to be over.

National Calamity

Then, early in the morning of October 6, news from the remote mountains of Guatemala started filtering out. Days of rain had fallen on the slopes of the volcanoes that ring Lake Atitlan, a popular resort 60 miles (100 km) west of Guatemala City. At 3 AM on October 6, while residents slept in the tourist towns and Mayan villages below, the waterlogged

Volcanoes ring Lake Atitlan, a popular resort 60 miles (100 km) west of Guatemala City. After days of torrential rain, mud poured from the slopes of the volcanoes onto the tourist towns and Mayan villages around the lake, killing hundreds as they slept.

hillsides began to dissolve. A half-mile-wide river of mud poured down from the volcanoes, swallowing at least four towns in a trail of sludge 20 feet (6 m) deep. Residents who had fled returned to find a field of car-size boulders where their homes had been. "There are no words for this. I have only tears left," said Manuel Gonzalez, a teacher in Panabaj, one of the destroyed villages. "There were only houses here, for as far as you could see. . . . It makes you lose hope. There are no children left, there are no people left."

Mudslides had buried more than 100 Guatemalan communities that week—near the Mexican border, 130 died when mud cascaded onto a flood-relief shelter—and several in El Salvador and Mexico. At first the authorities were unaware of the extent of the damage; the mudslides cut communication and transportation to the outside world. Rescuers rushed to as many sites as they could, but at least 90 lay beyond reach.

> "These are our brothers, our friends. And they're dead."
>
> —DOMINGO RAMIREZ, A VOLUNTEER IN THE SEARCH FOR VICTIMS

Entire Villages Buried

Around Lake Atitlan, Mayans stabbed at the baking mud with shovels and picks to unearth victims. By October 9, though, the task seemed not only futile but dangerous. "We are tired," said the mayor of Panabaj. "The bodies are so rotted that they can no longer be identified. They will only bring disease." The government agreed to declare the buried villages mass cemeteries. On fields of mud studded with iron rods that showed where dogs had found bodies, priests in traditional garb performed rituals for the dead. All told, as many as 1,500 died from mudslides in Guatemala.

The government asked for $21.5 million in aid from the United Nations, and helicopters brought much-needed medicine and water treatment equipment to Lake Atitlan. The far more challenging task would be feeding a population in which half the people go hungry in a normal year, now that 80 percent of crops were lost in some regions. "The problem is we have a certain number of people who have lost everything," said an American working near Lake Atitlan. "People who really didn't have anything to start with now have nothing."

Days after Hurricane Stan whipped through, the trail of mud that swallowed Panajachel, Guatemala, remains. Mudslides buried more than 100 Guatemalan communities during and after the storm, many of them out of reach of rescue workers.

Rescue workers negotiate a washed-out road in Tecpan, western Guatemala, on October 6, 2005. Earlier that morning, mudslides had buried villages around Lake Atitlan under up to 20 feet (6 m) of sludge.

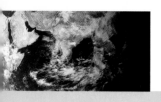

El Niño

SPECIFICATIONS

1982 EL NIÑO EVENT
Total deaths: 2,000
Worldwide damages: $13 million to $15 million
Flood damage in Peru: $650 million
Flood deaths in Peru and Ecuador: 600

Peruvian fishermen first used the term El Niño, which means "the boy" or "Christ child," in the late 1800s to describe the warm ocean current that lapped against their shores at Christmastime every few years. For the next century no one outside Peru paid much attention to this phenomenon. But after a particularly strong El Niño took 2,000 lives in 1982, the concern of South American fishermen became a worldwide problem.

In a normal year the winds at the equator blow from east to west. This wind activity pushes the warm water at the surface of the Pacific toward Australia into a giant pool one and a half times as big as the United States. The warm water tends to evaporate into rain clouds, which is the genesis for Asian monsoons. But every three to seven years, in a cycle now known as the El Niño Southern Oscillation, the winds slacken and the warm pool starts surging back eastward. Not only does it bring the rain clouds along, but it disturbs global air currents, disrupting weather worldwide.

Worldwide Effects

The signs that El Niño would return in 1982 were small at first. In May, weather satellites measured a rise of one degree Fahrenheit (0.5°C) in the waters off the coast of Peru. Then, in July and August, the rain started. Although countries around the world suffered hurricanes and floods, the worst damage happened in the area that gave El Niño its name. Torrential rains hit Peru, Ecuador, and Bolivia in October 1982 that did not let up until the following July. In six months the coast got 100 inches (250 cm) of rain. The norm for the region was 0.24 inches (0.6 cm).

These six NASA satellite images show the levels of water vapor over the Pacific Ocean during the 1998 El Niño. Areas with a large amount of water vapor are shown in red; lower amounts are shown in blue. Warmer ocean water causes more evaporation and increases humidity of the overlying air, which breeds storms.

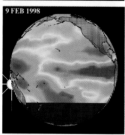
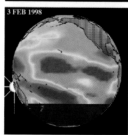
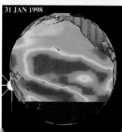
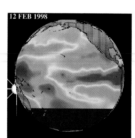
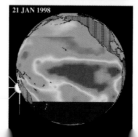

> "They strung ropes from one house to another to rescue people. Some spent 3 days on the roof. Those who knew how to swim brought them food."
>
> —MANUEL GUEVARA SANCHEZ, A RESIDENT OF A VILLAGE JUST OUTSIDE CHICLAYO, PERU

SPECIFICATIONS

1997 EL NIÑO EVENT
Duration: spring 1997 to summer 1998
Deaths worldwide: 2,100
Damages worldwide: $33 billion

Across the country, adobe homes melted and croplands flooded. The storms damaged water and sewer systems, so that many towns lacked drinking water. Mosquitoes multiplied in standing water, and related epidemics festered.

The ocean temperature off Peru finally returned to normal in November 1983. By then 600 people had been killed in Peru and Ecuador; 1,400 more died worldwide in floods, hurricanes, snows, and droughts.

The 1997 Event

Snow in Mexico, flooding in Poland, forest fires in Indonesia, cyclones in Madagascar—in 1997 and 1998, the planet suffered the frenzy of the strongest El Niño on record. Yet, as devastating as the storms and droughts proved, the number of fatalities related to the climate was roughly the same as for the 1982 El Niño. By early 1997 a decade of technological advances allowed meteorologists to predict the year's unusual weather with eerie precision. For the first time ever, afflicted regions got several months' warning of upcoming droughts and floods, and government officials took the danger seriously.

After El Niño caused flooding that destroyed most of the houses in their village, Chato Grande, Peru, the Yovera family evacuated to a refugee camp on March 15, 1998. The 1997–98 El Niño was the strongest on record.

CHAPTER 5

DROUGHT AND HEAT WAVES

SUDDENNESS SCARES US ALL, which is why citizens around the world clamor for preparedness plans against natural disasters—monsters that rear up from the darkness and strike before we can run. But what about the monsters who amble up in full daylight?

Whereas some storms, like tornadoes, destroy without water, others devastate with the abrupt introduction of water. Drought is the creeping, relentless absence of this essential element of life. The destruction comes not in a moment, but over weeks, even months, of shriveling crops and baking earth.

In a cruel twist no other disaster quite musters, droughts are viral and self-perpetuating. When vegetation dies and the ground dries up, no water is left to evaporate into the air, which prevents new rain from forming. In low-moisture areas, heat and cold are intensified, bringing even more misery.

But if drought sneaks up in plain sight, the culprit behind the recent spate of hot, dry spells has been an even slower burn. The implications of global climate change have been sneaking up on us for years, and the effects will continue to grow in the future. Crops, animals, and people dropped in the dry heat—just as they have for decades in China, Mongolia, Africa, even the Americas.

Left: The effects of drought are found in nearly every part of the world. Lack of water devastates crops, leads to water supply shortages, and contributes to famine. Extended periods without rain also increase the risk of wildfires. Inset: This world map shows average land surface temperatures between May 1 and 24, 2003. Temperatures range from black (coldest) to white (hottest). During this period, a wide area of southern India experienced temperatures as high as 122°F (50°C).

Right: Wildfires can destroy acres of forest, but they are also beneficial to the ecosystem.

Background: Heat waves and drought can ruin thousands of acres of cropland, causing millions of dollars worth of damage.

Below: Short grasses, small shrubs, and cacti can be found in most desert locations. The saguaro cactus is unique to the Sonoran Desert in the American Southwest.

Warmer World Equals More Fires

Damage to crops and livestock accounts for only part of the damages suffered as a result of drought. Lack of rain also brings destruction in the form of wildfires. In the mid-1980s the number of wildfires in the western United States rocketed to four times the average for the 1970s, and the blazes burned more than six times the area they had in previous years. Wildfire season is longer and hotter than it used to be, which may be linked to climate change.

DROUGHT SURVIVAL

As American gardeners living in the Southwest have been reminded in recent years, some plants are better adapted to drought than others. Desert plants survive heat and dryness by making the most of what is available to them. Succulents, like cacti and aloe, store water in waxy, nearly waterproof leaves and stems. Many desert plants breathe only at night, when cool temperatures and higher humidity minimize vapor loss. Some plants that have adapted to drought will shed their leaves, from which they lose the greatest amount of water, and essentially hibernate until the rain returns. Some animals, like the round-tailed ground squirrel, also hibernate through droughts. Desert animals sleep through the heat of the day, often under the sand. They are also experts at squeezing enough water out of their environment to survive—from cacti, insects, even seeds. Desert rodents have specialized kidneys to absorb as much water as possible, and organs in their noses recapture vapor in their breath.

REFORESTATION EFFORTS

The removal of forest cover impacts regional and global climate. Activists such as the 2004 Nobel Peace Prize winner Wangari Maathai work to protect forest resources. She formed the Green Belt movement, a grassroots, women's environmental-protection organization, in Kenya in 1977. Since then, the group has paid peasant women across the continent to plant more than 40 million trees.

Each year more forest is destroyed than created. The 2006 United Nations Climate Change conference estimated that 1.3 million square miles (3.4 million sq. km) of Africa must be reforested to make up for the destruction. The group suggested the planting of 140 million trees over the next 10 years.

Wangari Maathai, Kenyan environmentalist and winner of the 2004 Nobel Peace Prize.

More carbon dioxide in the atmosphere has encouraged flammable, nonnative grasses to grow in American deserts. But early springs are the true offenders. Air temperature defines the fire season at high elevations. A warm spring and early summer lead to acceleration of the normal cycle and a longer period during which fires can ignite and spread.

Fighting Drought

As efforts in Africa and China prove, fighting drought is an uphill battle. Planting trees and grasses shades the soil from scorching summer sun, but roots have trouble taking hold in dry, dusty ground. Thoughtful irrigation and river diversion keep water flowing where it is most needed, but the programs can be expensive and massive. Slowing global warming is an even greater undertaking—requiring changes in energy use from corporations to individual families.

An irrigation ditch provides water to a cornfield in the Arizona desert.

The Dust Bowl

Although they had been settled for decades, the Great Plains of the United States started to fill up at the beginning of the twentieth century, when railroad companies, state governments, and local boosters lured farmers with tales of luxurious chocolate-brown soil and cornstalks that stretched to heaven. The rain fails every three or four years on the plains, and a severe drought strikes about four times a century. But the settlers of the early 1900s, who arrived during a prolonged wet spell, assumed their good fortune would last forever. They found lush land, rich soil, and a giving sky, and milked them for one bountiful harvest after another.

Rape of the Land

Thus began the stampede to wrest a profit from the Great Plains. Farmers turned millions of acres of virgin prairie into cropland using techniques from the humid East. World War I drove grain prices to record heights, and 1920s technology multiplied the area a man could plow per day by a factor of 10. Using their brand-new mechanized tractors, farmers between 1925 and 1930 plowed an area seven times the size of Rhode Island. They were rewarded with high yields and higher profits. But once the Depression set in, wheat prices plummeted. To earn a

SPECIFICATIONS

THE DUST BOWL, 1930s
Area of Dust Bowl: 150,000 square miles (390,000 sq km)
Number of states affected: five (Kansas, Colorado, Oklahoma, Texas, and New Mexico)
Worst year for dust storms: 1937, with 72 storms
Topsoil lost in 1935: 850 million tons
Number of Dust Bowlers who migrated between 1931 and 1940: 2.5 million—with 200,000 to California
Government assistance granted: $1 billion in 1930s' dollars; $14 billion in 2006 dollars

living, growers had to sell more grain—and they planted the extra harvest on infertile land. By 1931 many plains farmers had a surplus they couldn't sell and owed the bank for their expensive new tractors. Meanwhile, one-third of the southern Great Plains—33 million acres (13.4 million hectares)—lay naked to the sun.

Nonhuman Causes

In an always windy region, few worried about the expanding spirals of dust whizzing by with escalating violence. Even in the summer of 1931, when the rains stopped and the sod dried up, farmers kept plowing, sure the clouds would come back. They wouldn't, though—not for eight years.

A change that had begun thousands of miles away in the Atlantic had an intense impact on the thirsty earth

"The ultimate meaning of the dust storms of the 1930s was that America as a whole, not just the plains, was badly out of balance with its natural environment."

—HISTORIAN ROBERT WORSTER

at home. Fluctuations in ocean temperatures weakened the flow of moist air from the Gulf of Mexico, which cut the rain over the Midwest. Then a vicious feedback cycle kicked in—no rain fell, so the soil parched; no water evaporated from the land, so no new precipitation formed. Then the ground simply blew away. Tilling and overgrazing had stripped the plains of the grasses that anchored the soil in place. When the wind picked up, it lifted huge clouds of now-dusty topsoil. "Black blizzards" blotted out the Sun and sprayed stinging dirt for hundreds of miles. In 1934, 100 million acres (40.5 hectares) of plains cropland had

A dust storm approaches a Kansas town in 1935. Experts later estimated that 850,000,000 tons of topsoil had blown off the southern plains during the course of the year.

lost most or all of its topsoil; 850 million tons of the stuff would blow away the next year.

Dust Everywhere

The storms left a layer of grit everywhere: on tractor engines, parlor floors, water jugs, cattle's eyes. Residents hung wet sheets over their windows, but the fine dust spilled through cracks in the walls. "In the dust-covered desolation of our No Man's Land here, wearing our shade hats, with handkerchiefs tied over our faces and Vaseline in our nostrils, we have been trying to rescue our home from the wind-blown dust which penetrates wherever air can go," an Oklahoma woman wrote in 1935. "It is almost a hopeless task, for there is rarely a day when at some time the dust clouds do not roll over.

'Visibility' approaches zero and everything is covered again with a silt-like deposit which may vary in depth from a film to actual ripples on the kitchen floor." Epidemics of eye and lung disease erupted—pneumonia inflicted a third of the deaths in one Kansas county in 1935—and patients coughed up 3-inch (7.5 cm) clots of dirt. The Red Cross distributed gauze masks, which accomplished little, aside from adding to the alien horror of what, by 1935, was called the Dust Bowl.

"If you would like to have your heart broken, just come out here," wrote a reporter in Kansas in June 1936. "This is the dust-storm country. It is the saddest land I have ever seen." From Kansas to Colorado, Oklahoma to New Mexico, farmers once lured by propaganda photos of elephantine watermelons, farmers who had celebrated bumper harvests a decade earlier, now watched crop after crop shrivel in soil dry down to the bedrock. Already poor from the Depression, many of them, after four straight years of drought, packed their cars and drove away. One-quarter of the population abandoned the Dust Bowl—the largest migration in U.S. history—many heading west to California.

A dust cloud descends on Stratford, Texas, on April 18, 1935.

Black Blizzards

Life in the Dust Bowl was described in the *New Republic* in 1935: "The impact is like a shovelful of fine sand flung against the face. People caught in their own yards grope for the doorstep. Cars come to a standstill, for no light in the world can penetrate that swirling murk. . . . The nightmare is deepest during the storms. But on the occasional bright day and the usual gray day we cannot shake from it. We live with the dust, eat it, sleep with it, watch it strip us of possessions and the hope of possessions. It is becoming real. The poetic uplift of

spring fades into a phantom of the storied past. The nightmare is becoming life."

Without warning, violent gusts would raise tons of dusty soil, enough to blacken the sky. Sometimes thunder and lightning cracked and boomed, other times the only sound was the howl and fizz of wind and sand. Gales and atmospheric electricity animated the dirt into sooty 8,000-foot giants that undulated and careened across several states, blasting away miles of cropland. One single storm in March 1935 wiped out 5 million acres (2 million hectares) of wheat.

Thirty-eight "black blizzards," as the storms were called, swept the region in 1933; in 1937 there were 72. Amarillo, Texas, suffered through 908 hours of churning dust in 1935, including seven complete blackouts, one of which lasted 11 hours. One storm endured longer than three days. Some stampeded as far as the Atlantic or the Gulf of Mexico. But the Dust Bowl's worst storm came on April 14, 1935: Black Sunday.

After more than a month of gales, the Sun finally shone the morning of April 14. Across the Midwest, grateful families poured outside to enjoy the nice day. But suddenly, around mid afternoon, a chill descended over the plains. With it came an eerie silence, followed by the frantic flapping of thousands of fleeing birds. Then a black cloud loomed up from the horizon, barreling forward at 60 miles per hour (95 km/h). Drivers veered off the road; one man was found the next day, suffocated in his car. Picnickers clawed their way across their own front lawns.

"My dad went into the kitchen when that dirt was blowing the hardest," remembered one survivor. "The wind was really whippin'. And I can remember my dad goin' in there and takin' hold of those two-by-fours and his hands would move up and down five or six inches, this wind was whipping so hard. And I thought to myself, 'This thing may blow away.'"

Dust Bowlers did their best to keep the grit out, lining windows and doors with rags, but to no avail. After a black blizzard, homeowners had to shovel dirt from their floors. Mothers fed children homemade concoctions to clear the dirt from their lungs—kerosene and lard, sugar and turpentine, skunk grease— and prevent the respiratory diseases that were killing by the thousands.

Roosevelt to the Rescue

Before the 1930s the federal government left emergency relief to local groups. But the national body-blow of the Depression challenged that tradition. President Franklin D. Roosevelt, inaugurated in 1933, ushered into law a series of programs and legislation, collectively called the New Deal, to get Americans back on their feet. Several initiatives were aimed at Dust Bowl farmers, including acts to buy surplus pigs and cattle and to protect farmers facing foreclosure. By 1937 more than one-fifth of rural plains families were collecting federal relief.

The Roosevelt administration also recognized the human hand in this natural disaster. Starting in 1935 the government paid farmers a dollar per acre to practice soil-conserving farming methods like terracing, crop rotation, and contour plowing. In 1937 Roosevelt introduced the Shelterbelt Project, in which the Civilian Conservation Corps planted parallel rows of more than 200 million native trees from Canada to Texas as windbreaks. A year later, the wind carried less than half as much soil.

As long as the drought persisted, though, federal aid could only act as a stopgap. Then, in the fall of 1939, real relief finally came—from the sky. "It was a very emotional time, when you'd get rain, because it meant so much to you. You didn't have false hope then," explained one Kansas resident. "When the rain came, it meant life itself. It meant a future." By 1941 rainfall across the country had returned to normal; at the end of the year, America's entry into World War II ended the Depression once and for all.

Rural resettlement administrator and member of President Roosevelt's drought commission, Rexford G. Tugwell, visits a farm near Dalhart, Texas, in August 1936.

Black Wind in Inner Mongolia

"Once there was fragrant grass everywhere, fresh flowers bloomed," reported a recent article in the Chinese Academy of Science's weekly bulletin. "Now it looks as if the land were suffering from a disease of the scalp." With each passing year, another 970 square miles (2,500 sq. km) of China's grassland turns into desert. Gobi sands sneak ever closer to the capital; one environmental protection expert guessed that "probably not long from now, Beijingers will go outside and catch a camel." A decades-long drought is partly at fault, but the bulk of the blame rests on human shoulders.

Sand and Wind

Just as in the American Dust Bowl, a glut of farmers using unwise methods has stripped the soil of the grasses that hold it together. Since the 1980s, farmers have cultivated more than 7,450 square miles (19,300 sq. km) in Mongolia and southern China; half of it dried up within a few seasons. Locals recite the common timeline: "Grasslands were cultivated in the first year, crops were planted in the second year, and deserts came in the third year." Overgrazing has harmed the land, with a domestic animal population three times the sustainable level in some areas of northern China, while reservoirs that divert the flow of Asia's rivers have also taken a toll. All these things, plus rising temperatures and vanishing rain clouds, add up to create a creeping desert.

Across the border, ferocious winds course through Mongolia. And as soil turns to sand, windstorms become sandstorms. Each spring, gales scour the bare ground, lifting tons of dust, silt, and sand

Northeastern China from space, March 10, 2004. A severe sandstorm sweeping southeastward out of the Gobi Desert is seen at center of this image.

SPECIFICATIONS

CHINA
Portion of China composed of desert:
27 percent
Area per year that becomes desert in China:
970 square miles (2,500 sq km)
Height of sandstorms: up to 2 miles (3.2 km)
Number of sandstorms in China between
2000 and spring 2004: 67

"Suddenly dust was everywhere—in my mouth, ears, hair, eyes and lungs.
Everything was red and all other noises drowned out
by the colossal roaring of the wind."

—AUTHOR MARK LYNAS ON GETTING CAUGHT IN AN INNER MONGOLIAN DUST STORM

as high as 2 miles (3.2 km). In the past 50 years, strong sandstorms, called "black winds," have developed with growing frequency. In the 1950s five of these storms occurred, in the 1980s there were 14, and in 2000 the country's media reported 13 storms. In addition to increasing frequency, the black winds travel farther now than they once did. Yellow clouds from Mongolia regularly blanket Korea and Japan, and in 2001 a storm traveled 7,000 miles (11,000 km) over six days to darken the sky over Arizona.

Recurring Problem and Possible Solutions

Sand has become a way of life in northeast Asia. In Mongolia it piles into drifts around tree trunks and building walls, and water trucks spray the main streets to keep the dust down. In May 1993 a wall of dirt 1,300 feet (400 m) high barreled southeast from Mongolia at 47 miles per hour (76 km/h), with winds as fast as 125 feet per second (38 m/sec). Children playing outside suffocated before they could get home. In all, 85 people were killed and 224 injured. The storm destroyed more than 4,400 houses, toppled crops, and killed 100,000 farm animals, causing $10 million U.S. dollars in damages. An even stronger squall devastated 675,000 square miles (1.75 million sq. km) of northeast China in April 2001, and in 2006 eight severe

Left: One method of combating desertification is to plant trees on terraced land, as these farmers have done near Yudushan in northwest Beijing.

Background:
The Gobi Desert.

storms hit—one of which buried Beijing under 400,000 tons of dirt—stranding cars and turning the sky yellow. "It is like going into a flour mill. It is hard to breathe when standing outside as the air is so smoky," said the deputy head of a monitoring station in March 2006.

China has invested $7 billion to turn desert back into grassland, although the ground is so depleted, trees and shrubs have a difficult time taking hold. Much more successful is the alert system the government unveiled in 2002. Using satellites and remote sensing, the China Meteorological Bureau was able to predict every storm in the spring of 2004; Chinese media have broadcast daily warnings since 2001.

Africa: Endemic Drought

The Horn of Africa—the jutting corner on the continent's eastern coast—hosts one of the most damaged ecosystems on the planet. Three straight decades of drought have stripped the overburdened land in Ethiopia, Somalia, and Eritrea of 95 percent of its habitat, repeatedly plunging millions of Africans into famine. Echoing the pattern that devastated the American Great Plains and northeast China, dry ground leads to dry skies, in a cycle that is difficult to reverse.

A History of Drought

Throughout history, droughts have plagued Africa about once every eight years, with the earliest recorded famine dating to 253 BCE. But since the 1970s, dry spells have smoldered hotter and more often, and droughts now strike every three years. This leaves the land, the wildlife, and the people almost no time to recover. Usually, the rainy season between February and June bathes the millet and sorghum fields along the Niger River and the carpet of grasses in the belt just below the Sahara called the Sahel. As they have for centuries, the nomadic herders of Somalia, Kenya, and Ethiopia follow the rains, allowing their goats, sheep, and cattle to graze.

When the rains fail, though, the green plains crumble into oceans of dirt. Plants wither, and the livestock that feeds on them starves. Between December 2005 and March 2006, 70 percent of the cattle in the Horn died, as did 20 percent of the donkeys and goats. From Kenya to Eritrea the ground was strewn with animal corpses. This led to famine among the huge segment of the sub-Saharan population that subsists on the milk and meat of livestock.

Widespread Famine

In the 1970s, 200,000 people starved to death during a drought in the Sahel. An additional 2 million died in Ethiopia in 1984 and 1985. By 2005 the Horn had suffered six straight years of drought. Corn and sorghum crops died, and by the next March, season after season of small harvests had put 6 million people at risk. Families in Kenya ate insects and squirrels to survive. Malnutrition rates in the Horn remain the highest in the world: 66 percent of Ethiopian children are malnourished. "If a doctor comes to our village and makes a survey," an Ethiopian housewife said in 1997, "he won't find a household in which there are people who haven't become bedridden due to hunger and disease. In some households there is no one even to give water to the sick members of the family."

> "They were mothers with children and babies . . . their faces were desperate, frightened. Death walked with them, close on the heels of starvation."
>
> —AID WORKER LYNN TWIST

SPECIFICATIONS

AFRICA
Number killed in 1970s' drought: 200,000
Number killed in 1984–85 drought: 2 million;
  5 percent of the Horn's original
  habitat remains
Percent of Ethiopian children who are
  malnourished: 66
Number of Ethiopians relying on food aid
  in 2006: 8 million

Farmers and herders responded by crowding into the cities. A quarter of the Sahel's population now lives in urban areas, and more migrants arrive each year. Refugees in the Horn flock to the Somali coast hoping to escape to Yemen and find work in Saudi Arabia. Few survive the trip across the Gulf of Aden. The metal skiffs they travel in often sink, and traffickers rarely hesitate to throw their fares overboard when Yemeni patrols come in sight.

Causes and Solutions

In order to alleviate the region's suffering, people are trying to understand the causes. Scientists suggest global warming and shifts in the jet stream. The effects of both of these natural phenomena are aggravated by the conditions in this land that is home to many, many more people and animals than it can support. Wide swaths of forests have been hacked down for fuel, and livestock have grazed Africa down to the bone. The soil has dried out in the sun, and when no moisture lingers, no new rain forms. This bare sandy ground also reflects most of the sunlight, causing the region to cool down, which inhibits monsoons. "Doesn't a person die when his blood is sucked out? It is the same thing with the land," an Ethiopian woman explained in 1996. "If a person is emaciated and

Even though Morocco borders on both the Mediterranean Sea and the Atlantic Ocean, there is always a threat of drought. On average, Morocco experiences a drought once every three years.

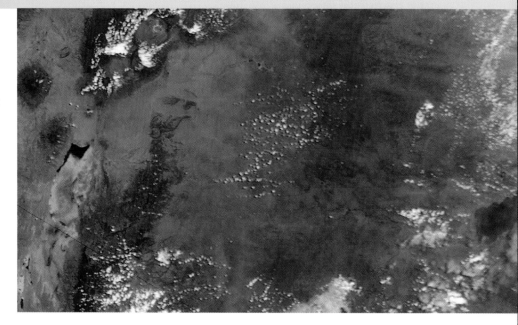

These images clearly show the effect of drought on vegetation in eastern Africa. The image on the left was taken on January 12, 2005, and the image at right on January 9, 2006, after a year of drought.

you push him, he falls down; it is the same thing with the land. It has now been weakened and does not produce food."

Droughts need not automatically lead to famine. But on a continent still struggling to vanquish the postcolonial treadmill of insurrection and civil war, stockpiling supplies and distributing aid have proven difficult. And just like the naked ground and cloudless skies, famine and social unrest provoke each other. Dwindling resources heighten tensions and push famished people to violence, while social instability hinders reform. Militias raid supply convoys and seize U.N. food shipments for ransom. Rustlers steal rival tribes' cattle, and farmers shoot each other over the

last scrap of food or the last ration of water. Meanwhile, humanitarian groups struggle to bring food supplies to the 8 million Ethiopians, 1.7 million southern Somalis, and 3 million Kenyans who would otherwise starve. Their handouts are at best a Band-Aid on a gaping wound. One aid chief in Nairobi likened food aid to addictive drugs: "It is addictive and creates an unhealthy dependency." Indeed, charity does nothing to halt the cycle of drought and expanding desert, overpopulation and poverty, disintegrating infrastructure and unstable government. But for many it is all that keeps them alive.

Long-term solutions take more time and energy. Programs to irrigate and reforest the plains are under way,

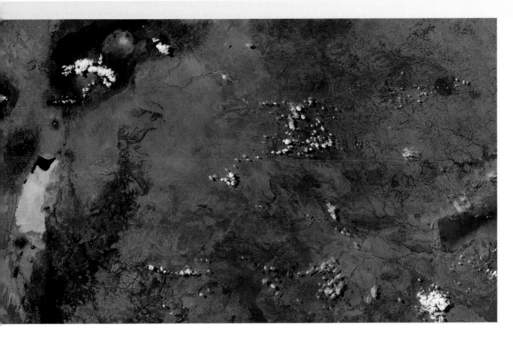

although the larger problem is not the number of trees but the number of people. Rural, sub-Saharan Africa has one of the highest fertility rates in the world. Many families have six or seven children, and only 3 percent of women in rural Ethiopia have access to contraception.

More important, though, for any reform effort to succeed, governments must be stable. If, as climatologists predict, global temperature does rise two degrees Fahrenheit (1°C) in the next decades, the lands bordering the Sahara will become less inhabitable.

PREVENTIVE PLANTINGS

To reverse the desert's determined creep, China has planted 12 billion trees in the last five years, and Africa is following suit. Trees block the wind from inciting sandstorms; they also prevent the soil from becoming sand in the first place. Leaves shade the dirt from the drying sun, and roots anchor it in place. By transpiring water vapor into the atmosphere, trees may even invite rain. However, in some regions trees may suck up all the land's moisture without encouraging precipitation. Research is ongoing to determine the impact of tree planting efforts.

Eucalyptus trees, which are native to Australia, have been planted in African grasslands for use as lumber, fuel, and paper pulp. Over time, the trees have been found to have a negative affect on stream flow and soil fertility.

Drought around the World

When the local forecast calls for a high temperature of 120°F (50°C), discomfort is expected. But when that kind of heat strikes a country on the tail end of a six-year drought—and where 70 percent of the population are farmers—discomfort yields disaster.

Years of Insufficient Rain

By 2002 India was suffering through its fifth straight barren year. Rainfall during the summer monsoons dipped 19 percent below the average. To the more than two-thirds of India's 1 billion citizens who farm for a living, the monsoons mean the difference between hunger and feasts. From June to September they typically provide three-quarters of India's yearly rainfall. Even the slightest shift from normal can wreak havoc. In 2002 the northeast and west of India flooded from too much rain, while the central and northern regions continued to parch. India's reservoirs held less than half their normal volume of water, and some had only 18 percent of their full capacity. Thousands of acres of crops withered, and cattle collapsed on the scorched ground.

For India's farmers and herders, the lean years took a heavy toll. Some villagers survived on wild grass, and half the children under five in one north-

SPECIFICATIONS

INDIA, 2003
Number of states affected by heat wave: 10
Highest temperature in Andhra Pradesh:
   124°F (51.1°C)
Number of deaths: 1,500 to 1,900

western state were malnourished. All hoped 2003 would finally bring rain. Instead, hot blasts from the Iranian desert fanned the worst heat wave in 20 years. From the second week of May to the first week of June, temperatures soared across 10 states. The thermometer hit 114°F (45.5°C) in New Delhi and 124°F (51.1°C)—more than 20 degrees above normal—in the eastern state of Andhra Pradesh.

Government Efforts

More than 1,500 Indian citizens succumbed to dehydration or heatstroke. The Indian government warned citizens to stay indoors between 10 AM and 5 PM and to drink plenty of water, but tin-roofed houses sweltered inside, and the heat evaporated the water supply. Brushfires consumed homes across Andhra Pradesh, and others regions lost electricity. Hospitals could not refrigerate vaccines or medicine.

The government, which had doled out $667 million worth of emergency aid to drought-stricken areas the previous year, now offered $214 to

"I promised to my children that I would bring something for them to eat in the evening, but I am empty-handed."

—Rajasthan villager to the BBC

So why had it been so hot? The cool, moist air that usually blew in from the Arabian Sea was blocked by ENSO-related sea-temperature anomalies (see page 104).

Left: Women and children standing in line for water in Nani Morsal village in the Indian state of Gujarat.

the families of each victim. Relief finally came June 6, when the monsoons hit the northeast. The rains—about a week later than usual—bathed a parched landscape and cooled the air. The Bombay stock exchange immediately rose 45.71 points.

This made way for the scorching winds from Iran. The tardiness of the monsoon prolonged the misery. Also, India has been growing warmer and drier for the last 20 years as part of the global warming trend.

A woman fetches water from a water hole in Bhathan village, India, in June 2003. Due to widespread drought, authorities were forced to ration water.

European Heat Wave, August 2003

In the summer of 2003, a massive heat wave swept across Europe. On August 10, England recorded its highest-ever temperature—100.6°F (38.1°C)—in Gravesend, Kent. Paris hit 100°F (37°C) and northern Italy 109.2°F (42.9°C). Dehydration and hyperthermia had already killed close to 10,000 people in France. Between 22,000 and 35,000 would die before the mercury dropped.

Hottest Summer in Memory

Summer 2003 was Europe's hottest since England's King Henry VIII was a boy. A ridge of high pressure was anchored

SPECIFICATIONS

EUROPE, 2003
Highest temperature in England: 100.6°F (38.1°C)
Highest temperature in Switzerland: 106.7°F (41.5°C)
Area burned: 2,498 square miles (6,471 sq km)
Total heat-wave deaths: 22,146 to 35,118

over Western Europe, blocking the usual Atlantic rain clouds and sucking in hot, dry air from south of the Mediterranean Sea. From Spain to the Czech Republic and from Scotland to Turkey, the continent began to sweat in June and did not cool off until mid-August. On the heels of a dry spring, strong winds and temperatures 20 percent above normal made a deadly combination.

The scorching heat stoked more than 25,000 fires across the continent, burning more than 2,400 square miles (6,471 sq. km) of forest. Portugal, with its easily kindled eucalyptus and pine stands, was hardest hit. More than 5 percent of its woodlands went up in flames. Eighteen people died in Portuguese blazes and thousands

Map showing atypically high temperatures across Europe. The colors highlight the difference in daytime land surface temperatures between July 2001 and July 2003. The red swath across southern and eastern France represents areas where temperatures were 18°F (10°C) hotter in 2003 than in 2001. White areas show where temperatures were similar. Blue areas were cooler in 2003 than in 2001.

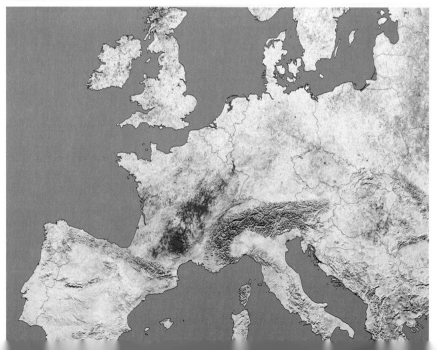

more lost their homes. The economic loss in Portugal alone would top 1 billion euros (US$1.3 billion).

The Destitute Suffer

Across Europe, farm animals and crops perished, train tracks buckled, and, while Europeans cranked up their air conditioners and refrigerators, rivers ran too low to cool nuclear power stations. But in France, a much more troubling situation was developing: The nation's elderly were dying from the heat, and no one seemed to notice. The heat struck hardest at those who lived alone or had no social network—that is, the poor and the old. Eighty percent of the dead in France were over the age of 75. And no one was home to help. During the month of August, most of France—including health-care workers and government officials—takes a holiday. On August 11 the public health minister was interviewed in the garden of his holiday home, assuring the public that everything was under control. By that point as many as 10,000 had died, and news programs were running shots of unclaimed bodies carted from empty apartments. The prime minister finally returned to Paris on August 14. The president followed on August 20, just as an incoming cold front (accompanied in France and Spain by severe thunderstorms) beat back the heat. By then 14,802 had died in France, and the public

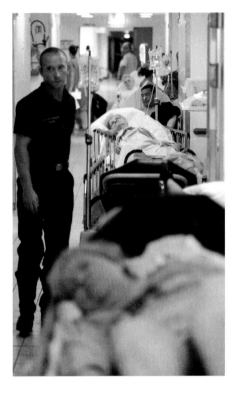

Saint Antoine hospital in Paris, France, took in many of the city's elderly who were stricken by the heat in August 2003.

was calling for the resignations of a number of public officials.

Across the channel in Great Britain the unusually tropical weather brought some levity. Britons jammed the roads to the beaches; bookies took a bath on wagers that the thermometer would never top 100°F; and swimming pool sales jumped 300 percent. Scientists ruined the mood by suggesting this was merely a taste of the future. A British climate research report warned, "By the 2060s, a 2003-type summer would be unusually cool."

Droughts Related to El Niño

Due to the shift in ocean temperatures as part of the El Niño Southern Oscillation in 1982, the giant pool of warm water that usually floats in the western Pacific Ocean started rolling toward Peru, dragging the monsoons away with it. The result was a prolonged, devastating drought from Sri Lanka to Australia. Between April and December 1982, most of east and central Australia received atypically low amounts of rain. Meteorologists proclaimed it the country's worst drought in the twentieth century.

Soil in Victoria escaped in the wind, and lakes and rivers shrank. Half the country's wheat perished in the thirsty ground, and livestock suffered. The worst came in February 1983. First, dust storms whipped the southeast, and then, in a tinderbox of dried-out forests and temperatures registered at

SPECIFICATIONS

AUSTRALIA AND INDONESIA, 1982–1983
Damages in Australia: US$2.5 billion
Area burned in Australia: 2.5 million acres
 (1 million hectares)
Buildings burned in Australia: 3,700
Deaths in Australian fires: 76
Area burned in Kalimantan: 7.9 million acres (3.2
 million hectares)
Damages in Indonesia: $500 million
Deaths in Indonesia: 340

Right: The island of Borneo suffered the effects of El Niño in 1982–83 and 1997–98. Wildfires threatened villages during both events. Here, villagers fight a fire on the outskirts of Balikpapan in 1998.

Background: Parched earth near Brisbane, Australia.

"The drought is not just a rural catastrophe, it is a national disaster."

—THE *AUSTRALIAN*

109°F (43°C), near-gale winds on February 16 fanned huge fires. The sheets of flame rolled across southern Australia for the rest of the month, destroying 2.5 million acres (1 million hectares) and 3,700 buildings, killing 76 people. In all, the droughts and fires caused damages costing US$2.5 billion.

Wildfire in Borneo

Thousands of miles away, Borneo's tropical rain forest was also burning. In 1981 Indonesia had produced enough food to feed itself for the first time in years. But when only a third of the normal amount of rain fell in 1982, reservoirs dwindled, wells ran dry, and Indonesians resorted to drinking from trickling streams. Famine, cholera, and diarrhea killed hundreds. Fires set by farmers to clear underbrush and weeds raged out of control in August, and the peat-rich ground ignited. Thick smoke reddened the sky, and most of the airports in Kalimantan, the Indonesian half of Borneo, shut down. Fire consumed 7.9 million acres (3.2 million hectares), about three-quarters of which was rain forest. Although rains returned to Borneo in May 1983, the forests on the northern half of the island burned until August.

Sheep seek out the shade of a water tank in rural Australia. The devastating effect of the drought on the rural economy forced farmers to kill livestock that they could not afford to keep.

INCREASING FOREST FIRES

The El Niño events of 1982–83 and 1997–98 ignited massive fires in the rain forest. This may seem impossible, but drought can make kindling out of a jungle. As the soil parches, plants absorb less water. When leaves wither, the ground—and everything on it—is exposed to direct sunlight. Soon all the usually shaded vegetation is as dry as paper, ready to ignite at the slightest spark.

And although fires may start anywhere at any time, the moist parts of the tropics normally need to rely only on their natural fire extinguisher—rain—for rescue. In times of drought, small fires rage unimpeded for months.

California Wildfires

As the summer of 2003 waned, the California Department of Forestry and Fire Protection worried that their state was about to explode. Fall is wildfire season in the West, and this autumn California was in the midst of a four-year dry spell. Millions of trees stood weak with thirst, their rusty needles dangling or lining the forest floor. Drought had turned 360,000 acres (145,000 hectares) of forest into a powder keg.

California firefighters excel at their jobs. They extinguish 97 percent of all wildfires less than 24 hours after they ignite and before more than 10 acres (4 hectares) are able to burn. But wildfires are nature's way of clearing out flammable underbrush and dead wood. By suppressing the flames, firefighters allow grasses, shrubs, and fallen branches to build up to dangerous levels. Because of a false sense of safety, Californians built their homes closer and closer to the tinderbox. Mountain towns sprang up smack in the middle of thousands of acres of dead trees, without a buffer zone between homes and land that was destined to burn.

The Fires Begin

Flames reported at noon, October 21, were the first in a siege. By midnight 13 major fires had ignited, and the next day, with temperatures hovering around

SPECIFICATIONS

CALIFORNIA, 2003
Total deaths: 24
Area burned: 750,043 acres
(299,485 hectares)
Total fires: 5,961, including 14 major fires
Structures destroyed: 5,394
Homes lost: 3,710
Amount spent on firefighting: $252.3 million
Damages: $974 million

100°F (38°C) and humidity down to 8 percent, firefighters were battling more than 150 blazes. Among them was California's largest-ever individual fire. At dusk on October 25, a lost hunter in the Cleveland National Forest in San Diego County lit a signal fire that quickly flared out of control. During the evening 340 firefighters assembled, but the flames were inaccessible in the dark behind rugged terrain. For safety's sake, firefighters would have to wait until morning. The fire, unfortunately, would not.

At midnight the Santa Ana winds—strong, searing blasts from the desert—fanned a forest fire into a firestorm. Walls of flame descended upon nearby towns, incinerating 13 civilians and one firefighter. Within 10 hours, the blaze had scorched 80,000 acres (32,000 hectares). Thousands of firefighters rushed to evacuate citizens and combat the flames. From just northeast of Los Angeles to the Mexican border, it was the same thing. Eight thousand exhausted

"I stepped outside and there were flames surrounding the whole neighborhood. It was coming at us from all different angles. We just started packing up as much stuff as we possibly could . . . grabbing every picture, every memory, everything we could think of."

—DUKE ADAMS, SAN DIEGO RESIDENT

firemen faced a writhing front
of more than 5,900 fires.

Worst-Ever Fire Disaster

The flames killed 24 people. Charred bodies lay inside cars or in driveways. People who tried to rescue animals or friends suffered extensive burns. Thousands of residents fled with pets and as many of their belongings as they could gather in a few sweaty moments. One San Diego–area couple ran for safety to their pool, where from beneath the water they watched their windows explode. Refugees slept in cars or Red Cross tents and wondered if their houses survived. A San Bernardino woman sobbed when she returned home to rubble. "[We've lost] our letters, our annuals and pictures when we were babies," she said. "It's not about the value of a washer or a Mustang. It's just about things meaning something because they are part of your life."

At the end of the month, cool, wet southwest winds lowered temperatures and dumped heavy rain over Southern California. By November 4 the worst fire disaster in California history was over, after scorching 750,043 acres (299,485 hectares) and 3,710 homes and causing $974 million in damages.

BENEFICIAL FIRES

"Throughout much of the twentieth century, park managers and visitors alike have continued to view fire as a destructive force, one to be mastered, or at least tempered to a tamer, more controlled entity," reports a National Park Service Web site. In the 1940s, however, ecologists realized that fires might actually have a benefit in the natural world. Parks began to let lightning-induced fires burn within certain limits, and the ecosystem flourished.

More than 300 natural fires in Yellowstone Park have flared without human intervention since 1972. In addition to clearing out wood that might fuel a larger fire, the small blazes may stimulate sagebrush, aspen, and willows to regenerate. Grass roots survive to spawn bushier plants. Some subspecies of lodgepole pine—which account for 80 percent of the trees in Yellowstone—rely on the fires' intense heat to melt the resin that seals their cones and thus release the seeds inside.

Receding Glaciers

The regal, glistening, blue-white sea has begun to sag and drool. Pockmarks mar the once glassy surface, and the dark rock face peers up after millennia under deep freeze. The Earth's glaciers are melting.

Glaciers in Peru have lost a quarter of their ice since the 1970s, exposing fossils that likely have not seen daylight for 5,000 years. One ice mass, Qori Kalis, now shrinks as much in a week as it used to in a year. Around the world, glaciers shed 22 cubic miles (92 cu. km) annually, twice the amount they did just 50 years ago.

Normal Patterns?

Glaciers have been melting since the end of the last ice age—millions of people around the world depend on melting snow-cover on mountaintops. During wet seasons in Peru, glaciers collect snow; as the year goes on, the glaciers release meltwater into the valleys, where it irrigates crops, helps power hydro-electric plants, and fills drinking glasses. In many regions glacial melt is the only

SPECIFICATIONS

PERU
Peruvian glacier area lost in the past
30 years: more than 20 percent
Area lost on Mount Huascarán: 3,160
acres (1,280 hectares), or 40 percent
Area lost on Yanamarey Glacier: 25
percent since the 1950s

water source. In arid western Peru, glaciers provide all the river water during the dry season and most of it even during heavy rains.

The threat now is that glaciers are melting faster than they regenerate. "You can think of these glaciers as a bank account built over thousands of years," said glaciologist Lonnie Thompson. "If you subtract more than you gain, eventually you go bankrupt." So what is it that is putting us in the red? Global warming. The industrial age has boosted emissions of carbon dioxide and other greenhouse gases, which trap the Sun's heat in the atmosphere. Average temperatures have shot up more than a degree Fahrenheit (0.5°C)

Right: The glacier Breidamerkurjokull in Iceland. Whether or not the recession of this glacier is caused by global warming is the subject of a heated debate.

Far right: Qori Kalis glacier in the Peruvian Andes, which is receding.

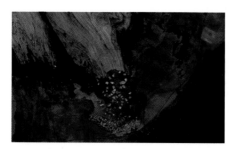

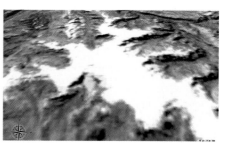

since 1900, the highest jump of the past millennium. If the trend continues, Earth's glaciers will soon disappear. The fabled snows of Mount Kilimanjaro could be gone in under 20 years, and the majority of the glaciers in Peru by 2015. "Once a glacier is lost," said glaciologist Bolivar Caceres, "it doesn't come back."

Impact in Peru

In Peru, home to three-quarters of the world's tropical glaciers, the loss has already hit hard. The desert country gets most of its water from the Andes, and some city governments already ration water. In Lima, the capital, 2 million people don't have water service; they pay private suppliers 30 times the going rate. If every home in Lima could pump water, there wouldn't be enough to go around.

During the dry season, when production drops as much as 80 percent at Peru's Rio Sante hydroelectric plant, Peruvians depend on glacial melt to pick up the slack. Meltwater produces 20 percent of the world's power. Fuel-burning plants built to compensate for the loss only compound the problem by releasing more greenhouses gases. Farmers, who struggle to keep up with an erratic water supply, watch warily as the white caps on the Andes shrink. The Incas believed the mountains were gods, and some Peruvians still consider the ice sacred: "When there is no water, there is no life, not for the animals, or the humans, or for the agriculture," said Peruvian farmer Emilio Himenez of the Llanganuco lakes region to a BBC reporter, in 2005. "I don't know what situation our grandchildren will be in."

A glacier in the Andes Mountains. Peruvians depend on seasonal glacial meltwater as part of their water supply.

DYNAMIC GEOLOGY

PART 2

CHAPTER 6

EARTHQUAKES

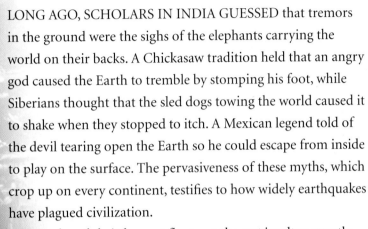

LONG AGO, SCHOLARS IN INDIA GUESSED that tremors in the ground were the sighs of the elephants carrying the world on their backs. A Chickasaw tradition held that an angry god caused the Earth to tremble by stomping his foot, while Siberians thought that the sled dogs towing the world caused it to shake when they stopped to itch. A Mexican legend told of the devil tearing open the Earth so he could escape from inside to play on the surface. The pervasiveness of these myths, which crop up on every continent, testifies to how widely earthquakes have plagued civilization.

Our planet's brittle crust floats on the semimolten mantle. More than 250 million years ago, all the land on Earth was packed into one huge continent, called Pangaea. Then convection currents in the fluid mantle broke the landmass apart and still propels the pieces today. The continents are drifting at about 2 inches (5 cm) per year, the speed at which fingernails grow. The plates of crust that support the continents ram into, sideswipe, and pull apart from each other, exerting tremendous pressure on the plates' rocky seams.

Left: Wreckage of a 21-story apartment tower that collapsed in the Mexico City earthquake of September 19, 1985. Inset: The line of the Atlantic fault is clearly marked by cliffs and ravines at Thingvellir, Iceland, where the North American and European tectonic plates meet. Pages 132–33: A steam-blast eruption emitted from the summit crater of Mount St. Helens in Washington State on April 6, 1980, about a month prior to the explosive eruption that caused the largest landslide on Earth in recorded history.

Below: A map of the Earth's tectonic plates. Red lines show where plates are moving apart, yellow lines where a plate is moving downward along an inclined shelf in the adjacent plate (hatches mark the down-thrown side), and blue lines where a plate is moving upward along an inclined shelf on the adjacent plate (hatches mark the upthrown side). Black lines mark other major fault zones (dotted black lines indicate that the fault's nature, location, or activity is uncertain). Red dots show volcanoes active within the past million years.

Opposite page: The San Andreas fault crossing the Carrizo Plain, between San Francisco and Los Angeles. The fault extends almost the full length of California.

Opposite page, inset: A geologist looks over seismograph readings from a recording station in California.

After months or years, the strain builds up enough that the slabs finally lurch forward, in what we know as earthquakes. Since the majority of earthquakes occur where plates meet, quakes help geologists define plate, or tectonic, boundaries. However, faults, which are cracks in the crust formed by the movement of chunks of Earth's surface, can run throughout a plate, not just along plate boundaries. Intraplate quakes, such as the ones that razed New Madrid, Missouri, in 1811 and 1812, have forced geologists to reassess these theories. But one thing is certain: When stress is exerted on a fault, there will eventually be an earthquake.

THE RICHTER SCALE

The Richter scale, developed in 1935 by seismologist Charles Richter, measures an earthquake's magnitude, or the energy it releases. Using seismographs, geologists can determine the height of the waves a quake sends through the ground; from those figures they calculate the earthquake's magnitude. For each whole-number increase on the Richter scale, wave amplitude rises tenfold and total energy grows by a factor of 32. A magnitude 8 earthquake would shake the ground 10 times as much as a magnitude 7 event.

Below magnitude 3.5—with an energy release equivalent to 73 tons of the explosive TNT—tremors are usually not felt by humans; up to 6.0 they rarely cause much damage. Anything above 7.0 is considered a major earthquake and releases as much energy as the largest nuclear weapons. The strongest quake ever recorded—in Chile in 1960—came in at magnitude 9.5.

The Richter scale does not measure damage. Waves of the same size can inflict more or less destruction, depending on the ground composition and local construction.

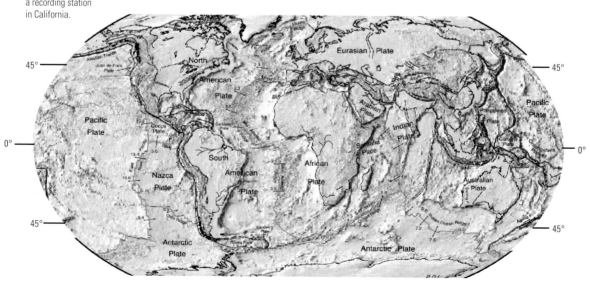

Problems with Prediction

When they strike, earthquakes are uniquely terrifying. So far we are unable to prevent earthquakes. Seismic waves travel from the epicenter—the point on the surface directly above where the crust began to rupture—at several kilometers per second, so delivering warnings once tremors have started is next to impossible. But geologists are working on ways to better predict impending quakes, giving people enough time to flee or take cover. Until then, preparedness—investing in sturdy buildings, disaster drills, and survival supplies—is the best hope for residents of earthquake-prone regions.

FAULT LINES

At a fault—a crack where chunks of the Earth's crust move past each other—tectonic plates may spread apart, or one may push over or under the other, or they may scrape sideways past each other. All these movements result in earthquakes. As the plates divide or collide, pressure builds. Earthquakes release the pressure—and higher pressure unleashes a more devastating quake. The crust bends under the growing strain until a piece of it snaps, allowing the plates to jolt unimpeded to new positions. Vibrations, called seismic waves, travel through the ground from the rupture. If the waves are powerful enough, they will shake the structures above.

The composition of the ground can abet or hinder seismic waves. Hard rock dampens vibrations, while soft sand amplifies them. That is why a magnitude 7 quake in one area might be more destructive than an equally strong event in another part of the world.

Pakistan, 2005

Kashmir, a rugged swath of mountains and lakes, is the object of the world's largest territorial dispute. Since gaining independence from Britain in 1947, India and Pakistan have fought two wars for control of the region. A border, called the Line of Control, now separates their armies. But a much deeper rift runs through Kashmir that divides two opposing subterranean forces, the clash between which jars both sides of the political boundary. The Indian subcontinent is crashing north into Eurasia at 2 inches (5 cm) per year, and an earthquake on the fault in 2005 killed as many people in an hour as the battle between India and Pakistan has in more than a decade.

SPECIFICATIONS

PAKISTAN, 2005
Magnitude: 7.6
Epicenter location: 50 to 60 miles (80–100 km) north-northeast of Islamabad, Pakistan; depth: 6.2 miles (10 km)
Deaths: 75,000 total; Pakistan side, 73,338; India side, 1,360
Area affected: 12,000 square miles (30,000 sq km)
Population affected: 3.5 million
Severely injured: 69,000
Children disabled: 10,000
Homeless: 3.3 million
Damages: $5 billion

This composite NASA image shows the Tibetan Plateau, bordered to the south by the Himalayas. The plateau and the surrounding mountains are evidence of recent uplift (23.8 million to 5.3 million years ago) and the region continues to rise, in some places more than 0.39 inches (1 cm) per year.

Crash of Continents

India has been slamming into Asia for 40 million years. When two huge masses collide, even in slow motion, there is bound to be some crumpling. In this case, the crash site buckled to form the Himalayas and the Tibetan plateau. As the plates continued to scrape against each other, pressure built in the fault that runs along the southern edge of the mountains. By 2005 the leaders on the Indian subcontinent knew the risks posed by the very earth beneath them. But India and Pakistan faced overwhelming, immediate problems—poverty, dirty drinking water, power shortages—that outweighed preparation for a hypothetical disaster. So when the threat became reality, most residents of Kashmir lived in dwellings of mud and corrugated iron. For tens of thousands, those shacks became their graves.

"We went down to the school and I saw my brothers lying there with their heads smashed. I felt as if I was losing pieces of my own heart."

—Abdul Qadir, survivor

At 8:30 AM on October 8, 2005, as the region's schoolchildren were sitting down at their desks, the ground convulsed. Six miles (10 km) below Muzaffarabad, the capital of Pakistani Kashmir, a 7.6 magnitude earthquake boiled up to rattle an area of 12,000 square miles (30,000 sq. km), from Afghanistan to Bangladesh. "The earth was shaking," said a 10-year-old Pakistani schoolgirl. "We were stumbling, we fell, we stood up and then we fell." Eighteen thousand children died, many of them when their schools collapsed. Those who survived found rubble where their houses had been. Some stumbled home to discover the bodies of their parents. "Everybody was running, screaming. I didn't know what was happening," said a Pakistani boy. He was orphaned that day.

The quake razed entire towns and killed 75,000 people. In one area of Kashmir, 95 percent of the mud dwellings had crumbled; in Muzaffarabad, two-thirds of the buildings were damaged. Substantial public facilities had failed, including 6,000 schools and at least three hospitals. The collapse of a 10-story apartment building in Islamabad killed close to a hundred people. Landslides swallowed other villages, and blood-caked refugees slept in the streets rather than risk being indoors during one of the day's 22 aftershocks. By the end of the month, a thousand smaller tremors had compounded the $5 billion in damages.

Help Arrives, Slowly

Military rescue crews immediately began to pull victims from the rubble, but they could not reach everyone in time. One Indian mountain village, perched just above a military base, languished with absolutely no help for five days. After 72 hours with no word from the army, locals in Muzaffarabad used a car jack to free a corpse from a block of concrete in a ruined hotel. One village schoolteacher trekked to the Pakistani city of Balakot four days after the quake to beg the soldiers there to help him save his young students. But Balakot had been flattened, and the army had only just arrived. The rescuers were unable to leave.

A U.S. Army helicopter delivering supplies to Balakot, Pakistan, as part of the multinational humanitarian aid effort that followed the 2005 earthquake.

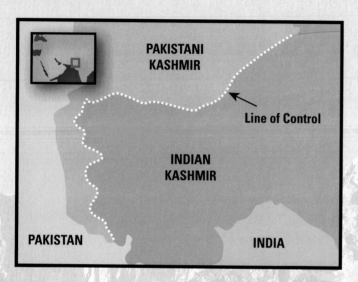

The Line of Control (dotted line) divides the administration of Kashmir between India and Pakistan. Kashmir suffered a severe loss of life in the 2005 earthquake with as many as 1,200 fatalities on the Indian side of the Line of Control and close to 87,000 on the Pakistani side.

prayed for help. But landslides had blocked roads, and the rugged hillsides offered no place for relief helicopters to land. Kashmiris designated helipads with big H's made from stones, but in some cases supplies had to be carried in on the backs of donkeys. The residents of Panj Kot, just inside the border of Pakistani Kashmir, had to wait until October 20 for their first food drop. When the choppers finally arrived, villagers battled one another for scraps or tried to escape on the departing aircraft's skids. Some villages did not receive aid until December.

Hope for Reconciliation

As the days turned into weeks, a greater challenge emerged: sheltering the survivors. The quake had destroyed the homes of more than 3 million people just as the bitter Himalayan winter loomed. Doctors soon began to see burn victims who had tried to heat their tents. The United Nations pleaded for $550 million in donations, but international donors were spent from a year of tragedy—Pakistanis had the misfortune to suffer their disaster just months after Hurricane Katrina and the Indian Ocean tsunami.

Meanwhile, hopes that the plight shared by India and Pakistan might spur them to reconcile foundered. Indian leaders balked at opening the

In both India and Pakistan, citizens accused the army of helping its allies first. Others blamed President Pervez Musharraf of Pakistan for hesitating too long—30 days—before seeking international assistance. The United States did finally send eight helicopters to aid in rescue and relief, but the longer the victims waited, the higher the death toll climbed. Thousands of civilians took matters into their own hands, traveling to the mountains with picks and shovels to rescue survivors. One man dug for three days, using only his hands, through the rubble of his sister's house before he found her, cradling her baby in her arms, both of them dead.

Relief proved equally elusive for the remote mountain hamlets. As food stocks dwindled, stranded villagers

Line of Control to divided families and relief workers, although they did eventually allow five crossing points. Militant Pakistani groups fired on Indian troops working to rescue victims. In a bit of bitter symbolism, the quake so weakened the Peace Bridge—which connects Indian and Pakistani Kashmir—that it closed to traffic.

A year later, although the debris had been cleared, rebuilding proceeded slowly. The Pakistani government doled out $44 million to the homeless, but in October 2006 most survivors still lived in temporary shelters; 400,000 slept in tents. If the quake had an upside, it was that 4,300 schools reopened immediately afterward, many enrolling girls who had never attended school before.

These two images show an area about 6 miles (10 km) southwest of the October 9 earthquake's epicenter before (bottom) and after (top) a landslide devastated the region. Debris from the landslide sent a shower of grayish rock into the Neelum River, turning the water from blue to brown. Background: The Kashmir Himalayas. Millions of years of tectonic activity created the Himalayan mountain range. Activity during the Pleistocene epoch (1.6 million to 10,000 years ago) caused uplift that made these the highest mountains on Earth.

THE GREAT TOKYO FIRE OF 1923

Four tectonic plates collide around Japan, making it one of the planet's most earthquake-prone nations. Minor tremors shake the country every day, and the record of major quakes goes back to at least 684 CE. The quake that struck just before noon on September 1, 1923, was not Japan's strongest, but it was one of the most destructive in the nation's history.

In addition to flattening cities and towns for hundreds of miles, the 8.3 magnitude temblor ruptured municipal gas lines. Fire burned much of Yokohama and most of Tokyo; between the quake and the flames, 60 percent of Tokyo was razed. About 100,000 people died, with 40,000 more missing and as many homeless.

Izmit, Turkey, 1999

Turkey is being pinched. As the Arabian and African landmasses nudge north against Eurasia, they wedge Turkey between them, inflicting an unending series of earthquakes on the Texas-size nation. A 1939 shock on the northern Anatolian fault, which runs 1,000 miles (1,600 km) from eastern Turkey to Greece, killed 33,000 people. In the next six decades, 12 more major tremors would jar the region.

When disaster hits a city, it wields a chilling potential for massive destruction. For urban areas along fault lines, earthquake-proof structures offer the only protection against the inevitable. Turkey, with its long history of quakes both major and minor, has passed a string of strict building codes. But laws protect no

one if they are not enforced, as thousands of Turks learned in 1999.

Rubble-Strewn City Blocks

On August 17 of that year, at 3:02 AM, an earthquake ripped through northwestern Turkey. Starting 7 miles (1.6 km) southeast of the city of Izmit, the quake rattled china cabinets from Ankara to Ukraine, pulverizing the country's most densely populated, industrialized region. In the 45 seconds of shaking, more than 77,000 homes dissolved into heaps of fractured concrete and twisted metal. Residents were jostled awake in bed to find the ceiling collapsing on top of them. Once the ground stilled, bloody survivors staggered into streets lined with rows of rubble where a minute earlier apartment blocks had stood.

The hot August Sun rose that morning on a scene of ruin. In Izmit and Istanbul and for hundreds of square miles, disembodied voices begged

Sakarya, Turkey, to the east of Izmit, suffered great losses from the 1999 earthquake. This building collapsed because the soil below it was unstable. The surrounding buildings managed to avoid damage.

for help from below jagged mountains of debris. Turkey had no rescue service, but search teams from Europe, the United States, and even Greece, Turkey's age-old enemy, flocked in with scent hounds and fiber-optic equipment. For victims buried alive under tons of rubble, every moment counted, but help often came too late. For every panting survivor that crews plucked from the debris, a desperate parent or child heard the tapping or crying coming from inside the ruins of their homes slowly fade. "We had to stand bodily in the road to get one [member of a rescue team] to stop and help us," said a Golcuk man whose cousin had been buried under a seven-story apartment building. Finally, a French crew pried away the concrete slabs to find the cousin still alive after 84 hours.

A mosque remained standing as almost everything around it was reduced to rubble in the August 19 earthquake.

WHY HAS THE MOSQUE IN GOLCUK SURVIVED?

Earthquakes are capricious. They can devour entire blocks while leaving buildings across the street intact. After the Izmit quake, the 700-year-old mosque in Golcuk, Turkey, made an enduring image, standing unmolested—all the way up to its minarets—amid a sea of rubble. Why did it survive when its neighbors collapsed?

Although some people credited the protective hand of God, several other mosques in Turkey suffered damage. Structural engineers suspect the mosque was simply stronger than the structures around it. For one thing, its neighbors were, for the most part, shoddily built. Also, traditional Turkish architects knew how to bind stone and wooden beams so that the building flexed as a unit, rather than splintering apart.

Mexico, September 19, 1985

At 7:18 AM on September 19, 1985, Andrea Dabrowski, a reporter for *Time* magazine in Mexico City, suddenly became disoriented. "I thought I was sick," she said. "There was this terrible dizzy feeling." As she stumbled to her door, she realized she was not ill. "The buildings across the street were swaying, really swaying. It was like being rocked in a boat. There were all these sounds of cracking and crackling, and the electric lines popping. I yelled out, 'God save me!'"

The solidity of the ground beneath our feet feels so basic, so unquestionable, that when it fails, we question ourselves. If the earth seems to lurch, we must be hungry or have vertigo or the flu. Unfortunately, Dabrowski's senses had not abandoned her that morning. Mexico had just suffered its worst earthquake in decades.

Thousand-Mile Shock Waves

Seismologists had feared a quake was coming. The nearby fault, perhaps the deadliest in the Western Hemisphere, had been quiet for far too long. A section of the Pacific seafloor is ramming into a westward-drifting North America. Friction locks the plates together where they meet, but the masses continue to shove. On September 19, 1985, the rocky boundary finally shattered. Starting in the

SPECIFICATIONS

MEXICO, 1985
Magnitude: 8.1
Duration: 50 seconds
Area affected: 319,000 square miles
   (825,000 sq km)
Population affected: 20 million
Deaths: 10,000 to 35,000
Injuries: 30,000 to 50,000
Homeless: 250,000
Financial losses: $5 billion
Buildings damaged in Mexico City: 412
Buildings destroyed in Mexico City: 3,124

Pacific Ocean 150 miles (240 km) from Acapulco, the ocean plate jumped forward 10 feet (3 m), sending shock waves over thousands of miles.

The earthquake measured 8.1 on the Richter scale, jostling skyscrapers in Houston, 900 miles (1,500 km) north, and in Guatemala City, 621 miles (1,000 km) south. Well water sloshed in Missouri and Maryland, and a tsunami crashed ashore in El Salvador. Some 20 million people felt the earth twitch, but the worst devastation struck southwestern Mexico, particularly Mexico City.

The capital was the world's most populous city, with 18 million people—a quarter of the country's entire population—living in just 890 square miles (2,300 sq. km). That Thursday morning, rush-hour traffic clogged the streets and half a million commuters jammed the subway. Then, suddenly, a thunderous roar erupted from the earth. Lamps began swinging, roads undulated, and buildings shimmied.

Others recognized their peril. A woman celebrating her birthday at an Acapulco hotel watched the wall "just crack straight down from the ceiling to the floor. The noise was terrible. It was the longest minute and a half of my life. I thought, 'This is it; I made it to 24 and now it's all over.'"

Haphazard Destruction

Across the city at least 412 buildings collapsed completely; 3,124 more suffered severe damage. "It looked as if a giant foot had stepped on the buildings," commented the U.S. ambassador. Structures between 8 and 18 stories proved most likely to fail; their heights allowed them to resonate with the shock wave. As in Turkey, substandard construction and building code violations doomed many buildings, but others survived. The city's two tallest buildings came through unharmed. Throughout the country, the pattern of destruction was haphazard: Hundred-foot mountains of rubble—all that remained of many apartment blocks, office towers, and hotels—were surrounded by intact buildings.

As pedestrians stared nervously at leaning skyscrapers and violent aftershocks surged, 10,000 Mexican soldiers—joined within days by crews from the United States, Great Britain, France, Italy, Canada, Switzerland, and West Germany—began to tunnel through the debris to extract survivors. Rescue crews strained over the noise of traffic to hear cries for help; once they pinpointed sounds, they often had to pry away gnarled girders, mounds of concrete, and corpses to reach the living. Doctors administered IVs while patients were still trapped in the rubble; often victims' limbs had to be amputated before they could be freed. Bystanders and volunteers cheered when rescuers emerged with survivors. After a week, the stench of decay pervaded the hot days, but crews continued digging.

Above: An apartment building in Mexico City. Many city residents were trapped inside the thousands of buildings that were destroyed in the earthquake.

Opposite page: A view of Mexico City in June 2002. The Aztecs built the original city, called Tenochtitlan, on an island within a lake. The lake eventually dried out and the city expanded over the empty lake bed. The soft subsoil is highly unstable, which has led to heavy damage from earthquakes and the gradual sinking of some sections of the city.

Rescue Effort Criticized

By the time the cries for help dwindled, at least 10,000 people—some sources estimate as many as 35,000—had died. Between 30,000 and 50,000 more were injured, and 250,000 were left homeless. Damages reached $5 billion, a towering sum for a country already plagued by unemployment, poverty, and the falling peso. Now, as hundreds of tents carpeted Mexico City's parks, citizens blamed the government for mishandling the rescue effort. Some accused President Miguel de la Madrid of balking in the face of tragedy. "In situations like this, every minute counts," a senior official allowed, "and we lost many, many minutes." Crews from Europe, on the other hand, complained that Mexican officials tried to prevent corpses from infecting the city by bulldozing rubble that still entombed survivors.

Over the next few years, though, the city would recover. The government of Mexico used a loan of $400 million from the World Bank to build new homes for 78,000 families and make 3,000 schools more resistant to earthquake damage. By just a month after the quake, traffic was moving and people were returning to work. A pall still hangs over the city, though: the knowledge that the 1985 quake will someday pale before the "big one" that awaits.

Built on Gelatin

Mexico City, 200 miles (320 km) inland, fared much worse in the

This eight-story structure broke in two and separated from its foundation as a result of the September 19 earthquake.

Several of the upper floors of the Mexican Ministry of Telecommunications office building collapsed. The 1985 earthquake cut telephone service and television broadcasts in much of the city. Many of the early reports of the disaster came from Guatemala.

September 19, 1985, earthquake than did Acapulco, only 150 miles (240 km) from the ocean-floor epicenter, and coastal towns like Zihuatanejo and Ixtapa. Even within the capital, the damage was uneven: Some neighborhoods stood unmolested, while the business district lay in a heap of dusty ruin. Some of the guilt lay with lax building regulations, but geologists blamed the ground itself.

Whereas the shoreline's solid bedrock anchored the coastal towns during the quake, Mexico City rests on an ancient lake bed. Some 30 million years ago an inland plateau rose in central Mexico; volcanic eruptions then hollowed it into a basin. The basin collected rainfall, and the Aztecs named it Lake Texcoco. Capitalizing on the water's defensive properties, the Aztecs built their capital on an island in the lake. Texcoco Lake dried up, and the metropolis expanded to become what we know today as Mexico City. North America's most populous city stood on spongy sediment. The capital has actually been sinking into the soft, damp silt at a rate of 10 inches (25 cm) a year, in some places at a slant, placing extra stress on already flimsy foundations.

Sandy soil is a welcome haven for seismic waves. Just like ripples on a pond, seismic waves undulate through the ground, and just like sound waves, seismic waves are affected by the substances they travel through. Voices sound different through a wall because the panels and studs muffle vibrations. The same sort of thing happens to seismic waves in the Earth's crust. Shock waves that had weakened as they traveled through rocky central Mexico revived once they reached Mexico City. The soft sediment of the lake bed jiggled like a massive bowl of jelly, which amplified the vibrations.

San Francisco, 1906

People who live on fault lines develop a curious mixture of fatalism, nebulous anxiety, and cavalier denial about the powder keg under their feet. In the past hundred years, science has allowed us to map Earth's hot spots and predict where big quakes are likely to hit. California, by all accounts, is long overdue for a major earthquake, but nobody can say for sure exactly when it will strike: tomorrow or decades from now. So Californians bolster their homes and plan disaster escape routes.

As San Francisco Bay–area schoolchildren practice ducking and covering and homeowners bolt their bookcases to the walls, they are aware that the worst earthquake in U.S. history happened nearby in 1906. People from Oregon to Los Angeles and from the Pacific shore to central Nevada felt the quake, but it was near the epicenter in San Francisco where the full impact was felt.

The city of San Francisco after the 1906 earthquake. The scope of the quake baffled geologists. The theory of plate tectonics was formulated about 50 years after this earthquake event, so the rupture, which we now know fell along the San Andreas fault, was a mystery to scientists at the time.

San Andreas Fault

At the San Andreas fault, which runs along the western edge of California, the Pacific plate is scraping north along the southward-moving North American plate. Where they touch, the two plates lock each other in a motionless shoving match for centuries at a time, until something gives and the plates move suddenly along their boundary, releasing hundreds of years of pent-up strain. When the plates slipped by each other in 1906, the resulting earthquake registered on seismographs in Germany.

At 5:12 AM on April 18, a foreshock jolted California from its slumber. Less than one minute later, violent tremors split the earth for 296 miles (476 km). The ground moved at 3 miles per hour (5 km/h), opening 20-foot (6 m) gashes in the bedrock. In some spots the landscape shifted as much as 20 feet (6 m) in four to five seconds, and previously straight fences suddenly zigzagged. "The noise [was] deafening; the crash of dishes, falling

"It was a strange San Francisco that I gazed upon . . . the grand old street was scarcely recognizable—a sad scene of destruction."

—CHARLES SEDGWICK

pictures, the rattle of the flat tin roof, bookcases being overturned, the piano hurled across the parlor, the groaning and straining of the building itself, broken glass and falling plaster, made such a roar that no one noise could be distinguished," remembered the wife of a San Francisco attorney.

"I never expected to come out alive. Stand in front of your clock and count off forty-eight seconds, and imagine this scene to have continued for that length of time, and you can get some idea of what one could suffer during that period."

The Fire

Sadly, the city had not begun to see the worst of the destruction in those 48 seconds. Over the next four days, flames would char 500 city blocks. The 7.8 magnitude quake ruptured several gas lines, sparking 52 fires around the city. Unfortunately, the water mains also burst, leaving the fire department with no means to fight the blazes.

San Francisco City Hall was destroyed in the 1906 earthquake. The new city hall building, which opened in 1915, was made earthquake-resistant after a 1989 quake damaged the structure.

ENGINEERING FOR EARTHQUAKES

Different building materials allow buildings varying amounts of sway before they break. Brittle structures will collapse under heavy vibrations. Each type of construction, from the small wood-frame home to the steel-beam skyscraper, requires its own approach. While many large structures, like the city hall buildings in Los Angeles and San Francisco, have been retrofiitted to float atop shock absorbers that isolate the structures from the ground, architects have learned to design tough but flexible homes by anchoring the foundations to the bedrock. Designers of large and small earthquake-resistant buildings avoid brittle materials like unreinforced masonry, bind the entire building together so it will flex as a unit, and add bracing walls throughout.

Background: Soldiers patrolling the ruins near Market Street.

Thousands of impoverished San Franciscans had been trapped when their ill-constructed tenements collapsed, and now countless victims burned to death before they could be rescued. Although the U.S. Army fixed the official number of dead at 700, recent studies have suggested that as many as 3,000 were killed in the quake and resulting fires. In many cases, entire families were incinerated, leaving no one behind to report them gone. The army dynamited buildings to prevent the spread of the fire, but to little avail. By April 22, 4.7 square miles (12 sq. km) of San Francisco—one-tenth of its area—had burned. Meanwhile, 225,000 homeless fled to tent camps around the city.

Displaced Citizens

The historian Bailey Millard wrote the following eyewitness account of the mass exodus from San Francisco:

> Headlong flight . . . in a thick, turbid desperate stream down Union, Green, Chestnut and other northside avenues until the crowds all met and fought their way down the crammed and choking throat of Bay Street. Never on Fifth Avenue or Broadway have I seen such a surging tide of humanity as that fighting its way down dusty Bay Street, past the shattered warehouses that had tumbled their heaps of bricks into the road and piled the way with masses of fallen timber. Automobiles

piled high with bedding and hastily snatched stores, tooted wild warnings amid the crowds. Drays loaded with furniture and swarming over with men, women and children, struggled over the earthquake-torn street, their horses sometimes falling by the wayside in a vain effort to pass some bad fissure in the "made" ground. . . . But by far the greatest amount of saved stuff was being borne along on man-back and woman-back, and even child-back. I saw one little girl of six or so struggling with a big bag of provision, the sweat streaming from her little red face and her eyes strained and tearful.

Residents had grabbed what they could before fleeing town. One witness recalled, "One woman carried a parrot's cage in one hand, while in the other was a bundle of clothes, hurriedly gathered together. I noticed that the bottom of the cage was gone, having

SPECIFICATIONS

SAN FRANCISCO, 1906

Magnitude: 7.7 to 8.3
Speed ground moved: 3 mph (5 km/h)
Duration of shaking: 45 to 60 seconds
Length of rupture: 296 miles (476 km)
Maximum offset at the surface: 20 feet (6 m)
Area affected: 375,000 square miles (971,000 sq km)
Deaths: 700 to 3,000
Homeless: 225,000
Buildings destroyed: 28,188
Property damage: $400 million in 1906 dollars

San Francisco's Chinatown was reduced to rubble in the 1906 earthquake. After much debate about relocating Chinatown to a different site, the decision was made to rebuild in the original location.

doubtlessly dropped out on the way without being missed."

In the fall the army and the city erected in public parks shacks that rented for $2 per month for employed families, but it would be years before all the quake victims had resettled. Chinese residents, in particular, feared they would never again have permanent homes in San Francisco: Every single building in Chinatown had burned to the ground, and now nativist business-men hoped to develop the coveted real estate into a shopping district. Officials shuttled the Chinese around from refu-gee camp to refugee camp, before they were finally allowed to rebuild at the site of the original Chinatown.

The widespread destruction did have one benefit: the birth of earthquake science in America. Geologists rushed to record their observations in the days after the event, and the governor soon appointed a commission to compile their work. The commission's report, the first wide-angle, coherent portrait of an American earthquake, formed the foun-dation for fault research in California.

Intraplate Quakes: Shaanxi and New Madrid

The Big Goose pagoda in Xian. This structure lost its top in the 1556 earthquake but remains standing today.

China is one of the oldest civilizations in the world. For millennia the Chinese have maintained a written history, including accounts of their disproportionate share of the world's deadly disasters. Squeezed between three tectonic plates, China's section of Eurasia is riddled with faults. As India crashes into Tibet, and the Philippine plate burrows under the east coast, and the rising Tibetan plateau blocks free plate movement, stress builds up in the crust in mainland China, producing tremors that disturb the Chinese mountains and plains. China's earthquake records date back to accounts carved onto bamboo in 1831 BCE. Almost every province of China has suffered an earthquake, and in the last 500 years scores of quakes have devastated the country.

SPECIFICATIONS

SHAANXI, 1556
Killed: 830,000
Magnitude: 8.0 to 8.3
Area affected: 500 square miles (1,300 sq km)
Number of provinces affected: 212

The 1556 Earthquake

The worst, by far, struck in 1556. Under the long reign of the Jiajing Emperor of the Ming dynasty, the country was enjoying a period of relative stability. But on January 23, in Jiajing's 34th year on the throne, an earthquake that has since been estimated to measure between 8.0 and 8.3 on the Richter scale shook central China. The earthquake came, according to the emperor's archives, "with thunderous sounds, and fowls cried and dogs barked. . . . Either springs with fishes newly induced by the earthquake, or city walls and buildings sunk underground. Or flat ground turned to a hill; or several shocks in a day or shock all day. Rivers rose or overflowed, Mountains of Huayue and Zhongan shouted, and rivers were damned for several days."

People in more than 200 provinces felt the ground shake, and towns hundreds of miles away from the epicenter in Hua County, Shaanxi Province, suffered massive devastation. Trees fell and the ground cracked open in the hills and valleys. City walls, official buildings, temples, and dams crumbled.

In the 400 square miles (1,000 sq. km) around what is now Hua County, few people survived. The area was densely populated for its time, and millions of peasants had carved homes for themselves in soft cliff walls. The adobe-like windblown silt, called loess, that formed the cliffs is usually quite strong, but it liquefied and crumbled under the earthquake's intense shaking. The manmade caves collapsed, crushing and suffocating their inhabitants under tons of mountainside. In all, 830,000 people were killed, a death toll that makes the Shaanxi earthquake the deadliest ever recorded to this day.

Lessons Learned

For days afterward fires burned in the damaged region, claiming yet more lives. Now-homeless survivors slept outside; with no walls, they were vulnerable to the prowling thieves and looters. Aftershocks punished the remaining towns up to five times a month for the next six months and continued for five years. During that time, though, the Chinese deduced a great deal about earthquake survival. Residents of one western city began to build their houses from bamboo and wood, realizing that more-flexible structures might withstand an earthquake, or at least present less danger of crushing their inhabitants. Qin Keda, a scholar who survived the disaster, concluded from his experience that "at the very beginning of the earthquake, people indoors should not go out immediately. Just crouch down and wait for chances. Even if the nest is collapsed, some eggs in it may still be kept intact."

Faneuil Hall in Boston, Massachusetts, was built in 1742 and survived the 1755 earthquake.

BOSTON, 1755

In the wee hours of November 18, 1755, New England suffered the first major earthquake in North America's recorded history. Tremors had struck the Massachusetts Bay area before, as far back as 1558, but none had been this strong. Modern geologists estimate the quake's magnitude at somewhere between 6.0 and 6.5 on the Richter scale. Like their descendants at New Madrid, many New Englanders believed they were being punished for humanity's immorality. The Bay Colony's lieutenant governor called the quake God's "righteous Anger against the heinous and provoking Sins of Men."

More than 1,000 intraplate earthquakes have hit the region since the Pilgrims arrived, although none struck Boston as hard as the one in 1755. A quake that strong today might kill thousands and inflict millions of dollars in damages.

New Madrid, Missouri, 1811–12

On September 5, 1811, a comet illuminated the midwestern sky. Comets have long been considered ill omens, and this one—beautiful and spectacularly luminous—stayed until January. But for the residents of New Madrid, a bustling settlement perched on a high Mississippi riverbank in what would become Missouri, the future looked bright. The largest town between St. Louis and Natchez, Mississippi, New Madrid was a white clapboard oasis for the flatboats and barges that emerged from the wilderness of the Louisiana Territory. But within a year New Madrid would be all but gone. While its neighbors flourished, New Madrid today is famous for one thing: the earthquakes that demolished it in 1811 and 1812.

Months of Tremors

At the start of the second decade of the nineteenth century, the Mississippi River marked the beginning of the American frontier. Its settlers had plenty to worry about—disease, floods, and angry, displaced Native Americans—without the earth splitting open. But around 2:15 AM on December 16, 1811, the residents of New Madrid were jolted out of bed by shaking that rang church bells as far away as Boston. Some 200,000 square miles (600,000 sq. km) suffered heavy damage: The ground heaved, tree trunks snapped, and buildings toppled. "The houses shook very much," wrote one resident of New Madrid, "chimneys falling in every direction—the loud, hoarse roaring which attended the earthquake, together with the cries, screams, and yells of the people, seems still ringing in my ears."

These elevated cypress trees in Lake County, Tennessee, are evidence of the New Madrid intraplate quake activity.

The earth twitched and shivered for months. Between mid-December 1811 and mid-March 1812, 1,874 shocks churned out of the New Madrid fault, two of them as strong as the first, which was likely around magnitude 8. The citizens of New Madrid were nervous wrecks. Most people darted outside as soon as the shocks began and could not be persuaded to go back in, which saved them from injury in collapsing houses. Only two people died on land in the quakes, although scores drowned in the heaving waters of the Mississippi.

Seeking Explanations

Geology was an infant science then, and no one in the Mississippi River valley knew quite what to make of the tremors. One local hypothesized that the Earth was caught between the "two horns" of the comet. Today we expect earthquakes where tectonic plates collide, but New Madrid sits in the middle of the North American plate, not at its edge. The temblors there are called intraplate quakes, which account for fewer than 10 percent of all earthquakes. Geologists are still debating what causes them. Some theorize the ground is rebounding after being squashed by a prehistoric glacier, while others believe it is rupturing from the pressure on the North American plate. In any case, the settlers chose not to stick around to figure it out. By February most had fled the area in riverboats. A visitor that month found the town deserted but for a few French stalwarts, "who live in camps close to the river side, and have their boats tied near them, in order to sail off, in case the earth should sink."

Left: These trees were killed by sand deposits along the New Madrid fault system, which extends 150 miles from Cairo, Illinois, to Marked Tree, Arkansas. The fault system cuts across five state lines and crosses the Mississippi River in at least three places.

Below: The New Madrid earthquakes caused this landslide trench in Tennessee.

CHAPTER 7

VOLCANOES

THE SAME STORY REPEATS again and again across the globe, with the same tragic end. People discover lush woodlands and fertile ground in the protective shadow of a mountain. They may know the rich soil is a gift from the peak, which long ago showered the region with mineral-rich ash. The mountain is a volcano, but it is dormant. So after centuries of sleep, when the mountain starts to rumble, most of the people do not heed its warning.

The following pages chronicle six volcanoes that exploded to life after decades or centuries of hibernation. All the while, deep beneath their quiet mountain slopes, a vast cauldron boiled. Tectonic activity, in addition to inflicting earthquakes, feeds volcanoes. Friction and heat from the Earth's inner layers melt the edges of the plates. Since the liquid rock, or magma, is less dense than its surroundings, it rises, melting more of the Earth's crust along the way. As magma collects near the surface, pressure builds until the ground splits open and spills its contents.

Left: Mount St. Helens erupts in a column of gas and debris 15 miles (24 km) high on May 18, 1980. The immense cloud darkened cities hundreds of miles away and dumped cinders over 22,000 square miles (35,406 sq. km); three days later, systems monitoring air pollution detected the fine, windborne ash in several northeastern U.S. cities. Inset: Lava oozes from a volcano in Hawaii.

If the molten rock is thin and runny, lava gushes out in glowing, orange rivers. While destructive, these flows are easily outrun by humans. Thick magma, on the other hand, tends to trap a lot of hot gas as vapors bubble to the top. When the volcano can no longer contain the mixture, it explodes, casting lethal black clouds of stone and ash for miles. But eruptions are not a monolithic disaster; they frequently provoke devastating landslides, mud avalanches, and fires in addition to their hot blasts and lava flows.

The Italian photographer Giorgio Sommer captured this April 1872 eruption of Mount Vesuvius for a stereo-image card. The explosion that year was one of the volcano's five major eruptions since it buried Pompeii in 79 CE.

MOUNT VESUVIUS

The discovery of the site of Pompeii, the Italian city buried under 10 to 30 feet (3 to 9 m) of ash when Vesuvius erupted in 79 CE, was a boon to archaeologists. Lava molds of artifacts and people in their last moments have taught us a great deal about life in the Roman Empire, but they also provide a cautionary tale for the people who live in Vesuvius's shadow today.

More than 3,000 people were killed when Vesuvius shot out an ash column 20 miles (30 km) high, and another 3,500 died in a subsequent eruption in 1631. The volcano remains dangerous, as the collision of the African and Eurasian tectonic plates below its surface continues unabated. Scientists maintain a close watch, and although Vesuvius is not currently threatening to erupt, some 3 million people reside within its danger zone. Within 15 minutes an eruption could devastate the land for miles around, including the outskirts of Naples, destroying the homes of hundreds of thousands.

PYROCLASTIC FLOWS

Not all volcanoes produce the glowing, red lava flows most of us associate with eruptions; instead, many exhale dense clouds of hot rock fragments and searing gases. These clouds, called pyroclastic flows, descend the mountainsides at more than 50 mph (80 km/h) and can travel as far as 125 miles (200 km) from the volcano, leaving a trail of destruction in their wake.

The sheer force of their impact can knock over buildings and trees. Temperatures inside the clouds can reach 1,000°F (700°C), so pyroclastic flows easily burn forests, crops, and people. They also carry enough ash and rock to bury rivers and towns in up to 650 feet (200 m) of debris.

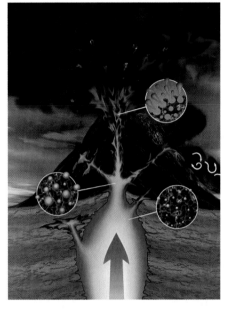

In this computer illustration of an explosive eruption, magma seeps upward through breaches in the solid-rock crust (lower center). If the magma rising through a volcano is thin, air bubbles at the surface escape quietly and easily. If the magma is viscous, the trapped gases explode when the magma reaches the lower pressure at the surface, blasting out a huge cloud of pulverized rock, ash, and lava.

While eruptions cannot be prevented, scientists are learning how to predict them. After Nevado del Ruiz in Colombia erupted in 1985, killing 25,000 people, American volcanologists formed a mobile team to monitor dangerous volcanoes. The work of these specialists, along with that of geologists around the world, informs locals when a volcano is indulging in some harmless huffing and puffing—and when they should run.

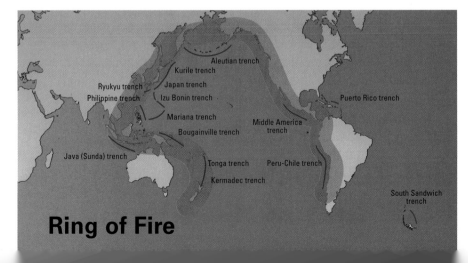

Ring of Fire

The so-called Pacific Ring of Fire, highlighted in orange, is a zone that stretches from New Zealand, along the edge of Asia, across the Aleutian Islands, and south along the coast of North and South America. About 75 percent of the world's active volcanoes are located in this zone. Oceanic trenches (dark blue lines) encircling the Pacific Basin form the ring, and volcanic islands are located parallel to these trenches. For example, the Aleutian trench is located on the ocean floor south of the Aleutian Islands.

Mount Tambora, Indonesia

Mount Tambora had gone so long without erupting that the villages in its shadow had begun to wonder if it was, in fact, a volcano. By the nineteenth century the behemoth on the Indonesian island of Sumbawa had been silent for 5,000 years. But in 1812 a cloud of ash and steam gathered around the summit, and a constant low rumble was punctuated on occasion by tremors that shook the island. One member of an expedition to nearby Celebes in 1814 found Tambora "in a state of great activity. At a distance, the clouds of ash which it threw out blackened one side of the horizon in such a manner as to convey the appearance of a threatening tropical squall."

The First Explosion

By 1815 the 10,000 people on the peninsula around Tambora were getting nervous. They appealed to the British contingent on the island to determine if the volcano presented any danger, and on April 5 a Mr. Israel arrived from the port town of Bima. Unfortunately, he had waited a little too long to launch his investigation. At the very instant he arrived on the slopes of Tambora, the mountaintop exploded, ejecting a plume of ash 15 miles high (25 km). Israel was perhaps the first casualty of what would become the deadliest eruption in history.

SPECIFICATIONS

MOUNT TAMBORA, 1815
Deaths: 117,000
Distance of ashfall: at least 800 miles (1,300 km)
Distance eruptions heard: 1,600 miles (2,600 km)
Pyroclastic flow distance: 12 miles (20 km)
Volume of ash discharged: 35 cubic miles
  (150 cu km)
Depth of ash near volcano: 3.9 feet (1.2 m)

More than likely the invading sea had awoken Tambora from its long slumber. Ocean water probably trickled into the volcano through cracks in the seafloor, where it was instantly vaporized by magma. Accumulating steam festered beneath the summit until it finally blew the mountain to pieces. The eruption on April 5, while only moderately explosive, was loud enough that people thousands of kilometers away mistook its detonations for cannon booms. Troops on nearby islands even prepared for battle, until showers of ash hinted at the true source of the sound. Cinders fell as far away as Java in a light sprinkle that continued, along with smaller explosions, for the next five days. Residents of Sumbawa, after their initial alarm, enjoyed the spectacular display, hoping the ash would fertilize the soil. But all this was merely warm-up.

Months of Activity

At 7:00 PM on April 10, a barrage of huge explosions fired three columns of flame, ash, and rock 26 miles (40 km) into the air. Twenty-inch (50 cm) pumice stones pelted Sumbawa, followed by winds strong enough to uproot trees and topple houses, cattle, and men. At 10 PM the massive black cloud collapsed onto the slopes, unleashing an incandescent river of soot and smoke. Tambora "appeared like a body of liquid fire extending itself in every direction," remembered the Raja of Sanggar. Moving at up to 100 miles per hour (160 km/h), the avalanche smothered the kingdoms of Tambora and Pekat in moments, killing every single inhabitant. It rampaged as far as 12 miles (20 km) from the summit, killing everything it touched and raising 16-foot (5 m) tsunamis when it exploded on contact with the sea.

The ash cloud blotted out the sun, thrusting most of Indonesia into pitch darkness for three days. "For several days after I transacted all business by candlelight," wrote a Scottish scholar and diplomat on nearby Surabaya. "For several months, indeed, the sun's disk was not distinct." The explosions quieted somewhat on the evening of April 11, although sooty clouds clung to the summit for weeks. The final explosion came in mid-July, and the smoke stopped spewing on August 23.

A volcanic ash plume rises from Mount St. Helens. The 1815 explosion of Mount Tambora sent up an ash plume 15 miles (25 km) high.

By then Tambora had expelled 35 cubic miles (150 cu. km) of ash in history's most powerful, most prolific eruption. Cinders rained down 800 miles (1,300 km) from the summit, and Sumbawa was blanketed up to 4 feet (1.2 m) deep. "Yesterday the ashes fell so thick," claimed a letter-writer in Java on April 14, "that it was quite uncomfortable walking out as it filled our eyes and covered our clothes." Surging lava had killed 10,000 people on Sumbawa instantly. Nearly two centuries later, volcanologists dug through 10 feet (3 m) of pumice and ash where the kingdom of Tambora once stood. In one collapsed building they found a woman "knocked over on her back by the force of the pyroclastic flow," said the team's leader, "and she appeared to be holding a machete or long knife in one hand. Over her arm was a cloth, and we think it was a sarong, totally carbonized." Searing gas clouds and missiles of flaming rock took 70,000 more lives around Indonesia.

A view of Mount Tambora from the Space Shuttle Discovery. The volcano's massive caldera, which was formed during the 1815 eruption, is easily visible even from this distance.

Life after Eruption

For those who survived, the next years would be a misery. On Sumbawa 75 percent of the livestock had died in the eruption, and carpets of ash smothered 95 percent of the rice crop and vast belts of forest. Residents of Sumbawa and the surrounding islands had subsisted on the sale of rice, timber, honey, beeswax, and horses, and without those commodities the economy collapsed. Sumbawa, Bali, and Lombok now lived on expensive rice from Java, but they had nothing to exchange for it. Tribes in western Sumbawa rooted in the graves of their dead for treasures to barter with, and elsewhere islanders survived on dogs, horses, and poisonous leaves or sold their sons and daughters in exchange for a meal. Some parents killed their children rather than watch them starve. Water that had been polluted by ash fueled outbreaks of diarrhea, and victims dropped by the thousands. Bodies littered rice fields, roads, and beaches. "The survivors are too weak and too few in number to pay the daily dying victims the honor of a funeral," reported a Balinese newspaper in October.

Disease and famine killed 37,000 people in the Dutch East Indies before farmers could coax crops from Sumbawa's ground, five years after the eruption. Chunks of pumice floated in the sea around Tambora as late as 1819, and ash and downed trees were strewn over a landscape rife with gaping fissures. In 1824 two Dutch officials wrote that where Tambora and Pekat had stood now lay a "desolate heap of rubble." Even the volcano was a shadow of its former self. The explosions had blasted out a caldera 5 miles (8 km) wide, lopping off a third of Tambora's original height.

The Year of No Summer

The eruption of Mount Tambora in April 1815 sprayed 400 million tons of sulfur dioxide up to 28 miles (45 km) into the sky. The gases spread around the globe, reacting with other com-

pounds high in the stratosphere to form a persistent layer that blocked sunlight. For years, the world was treated to beautiful sunsets, but the layer also left a more sinister legacy. In Europe and North America, halfway around the world from Tambora, 1816 was referred to as the year without a summer, or, as it was more colorfully known, "eighteen hundred and froze-to-death."

Ash spewed into the upper atmosphere by Mount Pinatubo in 1991 colors a beautiful sunset in Tamworth, Australia. Volcanic eruptions can release enough sulfur dioxide to interfere with weather patterns; Tambora's gas cloud affected temperatures and precipitation around the world.

SUPER-VOLCANOES

The 18-by-60-mile (30 by 100 km) Lake Toba, on the Indonesian island of Sumatra, is the most visible vestige of the largest volcanic eruption in the last 2 million years. Some 74,000 years ago, a super-volcano, fed by a huge reservoir of magma under the Earth's surface, disgorged 670 cubic miles (2,800 cu. km) of ash and rock, thousands of times the output of Mount St. Helens in 1980. Ash fell over an area of at least 1.5 million square miles (4 million sq. km)—half the size of the continental United States. The eruption most likely belched out enough sulfur dioxide to cool the Earth for years. When all of that material was ejected, the ground collapsed, forming a caldera. Rain then filled the depression that became Lake Toba.

Super-volcanoes also lurk beneath Yellowstone National Park and New Zealand, but devastating eruptions strike only every hundred thousand years.

Global temperatures fell as much as 5°F (3°C) in 1816. Worldwide, hundreds of thousands of people starved to death when harvests failed. Atlantic shipping lanes iced over and glaciers spread. In Europe, Canada, and the northeastern United States, spring came much later than normal, and summer brought only more cold and rain. Snow fell in New England in June, and frost sparkled on the ground in August. On June 5 temperatures in Salem, Massachusetts, fell from 90°F (32°C) in the morning to 41°F (5°C) that evening. As hard as North American farmers tried to plant viable crops, the frost attacked even the hardiest roots. The entire corn crop—a staple—failed. Food prices skyrocketed, and livestock that had already been shivering in the cold now

A molten boulder bulges from a lava flow. If the magma rising through a volcano is thin, air bubbles escape quietly and easily when the magma reaches the surface. If, on the other hand, the rising magma is very thick, the pressure builds up until the gases explode, often causing a pyroclastic flow.

starved—as did its owners. Famine gripped the young republic. For many northeastern growers, 1816 was the last straw. Tired of bitter winters and withering harvests, twice the usual number of farmers pulled up stakes and headed west.

From Europe to Asia

Much of Europe fell under the same pall. Brown snow—tinted by dust from Tambora—fell in Hungary and Italy throughout spring. Geneva, Switzerland, suffered its coldest July since 1753, a record that would stand for nearly 150 years. Harvests shriveled from central Europe to the British Isles. After 142 days of rain killed the oat, wheat, and potato crops, Ireland endured famine and an outbreak of typhoid. Germans baked bread from sawdust and straw. Constant rains flooded the continent. "The earth is so prodigiously

soaked," wrote a Swiss diarist on July 8, "that fountains emerge from every hole. Streams came into being where none had been before." In Switzerland citizens hijacked grain shipments from Russia or ate their own cats, and the government, in addition to declaring a national emergency, set up a program to teach the crowds trying to harvest moss to recognize poisonous plants. In France and Britain hungry mobs raided and emptied grain warehouses. The British government abolished the income tax for the duration.

The eruption also delayed the monsoons in Asia. The late rains caused a famine, which weakened resistance to disease, allowing an incipient outbreak of cholera to develop into a worldwide epidemic. Even as the climate ran haywire on three continents, no one recognized Tambora's role. In 1913 an American meteorologist demonstrated the connection between eruptions and global cooling, allowing scientists finally to finger the instigator in a worldwide calamity.

Above: Lake Toba, in Sumatra was formed some 74,000 years ago in a massive volcanic eruption. Although major earthquakes frequently occur in the area, this so-called super-volcano has not erupted in historical time.

Below: An artist's rendering of the 1883 Krakatau eruption. The volcano exploded on August 27 of that year with potentially the loudest sound in recorded history, heard 2,200 miles (3,500 km) away. After the eruption, only one-third of the volcanic island remained above the surface of the ocean.

KRAKATAU, INDONESIA, 1883

Powerful eruptions are almost always deadly in their own right, but they can also set off other disasters that kill many, if not even more, people. On August 27, 1883, after three months of steaming, the Indonesian volcano Krakatau (often called Krakatoa) vented 4 cubic miles (17 cu. km) of ash and rock in one of the biggest explosions ever recorded on Earth.

The eruption stirred up a 140-foot (40 m) tsunami that affected tides 4,000 miles (7,000 km) away. The tsunami submerged 165 villages in Java and Sumatra and killed 36,000 people, a death toll that made the Krakatau eruption the second-deadliest volcanic event in recorded history.

Mount Pelée, Martinique

After months of steaming, rumbling, and exploding, Mount Pelée was finally beginning to scare Martinique's most populous city. St. Pierre lay just 4 miles (6 km) downslope from the summit of the sputtering volcano, and as ashfalls and ground tremors chased rural residents into the metropolis in May 1902, Pierrotins were jamming the decks of ferries to the Caribbean island's capital, Fort-de-France. The editor of Martinique's newspaper saw the exodus as an act of cowardice tantamount to betrayal. "Do those who are invading Fort-de-France imagine that they would be safer there

SPECIFICATIONS

MT. PELÉE, 1902
Area of destruction: 8 square miles (20 sq km)
Initial speed of pyroclastic cloud: 360 to 420 mph (580 to 680 km/h)
Speed of pyroclastic cloud at St. Pierre: 100 mph (160 km/h)
Temperature of cloud: 2,000°F (1,100°C)
Deaths: approximately 30,000

than here . . . ?" he asked in the May 7 edition. His next question echoed the sentiment of 26,000 people who, unbeknownst to them, had just one more day to live. "Where better off could one be than in St. Pierre?"

St. Pierre was a picturesque port on a beautiful island, the social and commercial capital of a French colonial

"The city is covered with ashes. The smell of sulphur is so strong that horses on the street stop and snort, and some of them drop in their harness and die from suffocation."

—Mrs. Thomas T. Prentis, wife of the American consul in St. Pierre

jewel. Lemon-yellow stucco houses lined narrow, winding avenues with names like Climb to Heaven Street, referring to the green mountains that rose at the city's back. The highest peak, at 4,584 feet (1,397 m), was Mount Pelée. Its 39-square-mile (100 sq. km) base formed the entire north end of Martinique. The volcano had erupted in 1792 and 1851, but neither event caused much damage, and the unconcerned Martiniquois even picnicked on Pelée's summit.

Left: A 1902 photograph shows the view from Martinique's Orange Hill sometime after May 8. The once-vibrant St. Pierre was a blackened tessellation of charred buildings, with the still-steaming culprit looming in the distance.

Below: An avalanche lily pokes through volcanic debris in Skamania County, Washington—just 10 miles (16 km) northwest of Mount St. Helens—less than two months after the 1980 eruption.

VOLCANIC ERUPTIONS AND THE NATURAL WORLD

The surviving crew of the passenger steamer *Roddam*, which was anchored at St. Pierre when Mount Pelée's wall of fire struck the city, managed to steer their ship to St. Lucia. When port officials came upon the badly burned men, the *Roddam*'s captain explained, "We came from hell."

Volcanoes are hell on Earth, so it is difficult to imagine that they can have a positive effect on the natural world. Indeed, raining cinders can suffocate or burn animals, and ash on the ground deeper than 6 feet (2 m) will smother all plants. Gas blasts snap trees, and lava flows kill everything they encounter.

However, flora and fauna can prove amazingly tenacious. When the tops of plants are lopped off, they may regenerate from the roots and poke through the ash. Animals that hide underground, like gophers and ants, can survive lava and pyroclastic flows; their subsequent burrowing helps mix the ash with the soil to create compost that welcomes new growth.

Above: Ruins and debris in the village of Basse-Pointe, on the northern coast of Martinique. Soon after the eruption's initial blast, a downpour began to wet the rising cloud of ash. The boulders on the right were carried from the volcano by seething mud flows.

Right: A photograph of Mount Pelée's 1902 eruption. Note the ground-hugging gas clouds on the right; pyroclastic flows at 2,000°F (1,100°C) raced down the slope to snuff out the population of St. Pierre within minutes.

Then, at 7:52 AM on May 8, with a sound one witness likened to "all the machinery in the world breaking down at once," a cloud of black smoke blew off the south face of the mountain. At the same moment a second black cloud boiled up to fill the entire sky, plunging 50 square miles (130 sq. km) of the island into total darkness. Rolling downslope as if propelled, a roiling mass of scorching embers pummeled St. Pierre with hurricane force within a minute. Every single tree was uprooted and stripped. Masonry was pulverized. Barrels of rum exploded on the quay in turbulent, 2,000°F (1,100°C) gases. In

From Disbelief to Anguish

In January 1902 Mount Pelée began venting sulfurous oil. Beyond complaining about the stench, residents of Martinique were not worried. April brought earthquakes, ashfalls, and minor explosions from the summit, but a team of experts had assured the public there was no danger of eruption. But by early May powdery cinder had whitened the northern half of the island and deafening detonations were coming every five or six hours. Residents of St. Pierre crammed the churches seeking absolution, but for every businessman who packed his family onto an outbound steamer, many more rural families arrived from the uplands to what they hoped was safety in the big city.

Refugees gather on a street in Fort-de-France, which became Martinique's leading city after St. Pierre was destroyed. While only two survivors were discovered within St. Pierre, on the outskirts of the volcano's ring of destruction vegetation and homes were burned, but most people escaped death.

two minutes 26,000 people, their clothes ripped off their bodies in the blast, burned to death in St. Pierre; only two people within the city walls survived.

Four thousand more died elsewhere on the island. Survivors toyed with evacuating for good, but prompt international aid and a sense of fatalism caused many to stay. Today, St. Pierre has been rebuilt, but with only 5,000 inhabitants, it is a shadow of the bustling, vibrant city that was wiped out of existence.

FORECASTING

Volcanoes typically give plenty of warning—sometimes for years—when an eruption is brewing. In the past century geologists and volcanologists have become more and more adept at identifying and monitoring the precursors to eruption.

Magma forcing its way to the surface of a volcano has several measurable effects on the surrounding earth. The moving mass deforms the ground, which can be measured with a device called a tiltmeter, and disrupts faults, causing earthquakes. Keeping track of the frequency and degree of these symptoms can give scientists an idea of how close a volcano is to erupting.

Accurate predictions can save countless lives. For example, timely evacuation saved some 60,000 Filipinos when Mount Pinatubo erupted in 1991.

Soufrière Hills, Montserrat

Across the tiny Caribbean island of Montserrat runs a line that citizens are not allowed to cross. Since 1995 any unauthorized person who sneaks into the "exclusion zone" that covers the southern two-thirds of the British territory may be fined or imprisoned. The former capital, Plymouth, lies on the forbidden side of the line, its once-cheerful stucco homes and government buildings pounded into rubble, the tops of church steeples and streetlights poking up from a lake of muddy ash. Plymouth and several other villages have been abandoned because of their proximity to the growling, belching giant that glowers over the island from the south: the 3,000-foot (900 m) Soufrière Hills volcano, which has been erupting for years.

With Soufrière Hills visible in the distance, the empty buildings of Montserrat's onetime capital, Plymouth, poke through mud and ash left by pyroclastic flows in 1997. The city was evacuated before the eruption, so casualties were minimal.

Unstable Ground

Montserrat is one in a chain of islands formed where the North American plate slides under the Caribbean plate. The North American plate, dipping into the molten material below, melts and bubbles to the surface, a process that helped create the islands more than 100 million years ago. Apart from a moderate eruption in the 1600s, Soufrière Hills remained quiet for 10,000 years—until 1995. On July 18 of that year, it began rumbling and spitting steam and ash. Volcanologists detected sulfur dioxide, a sign that magma was frothing up to the surface. By mid-August officials had removed 6,000 ill and elderly residents to the northern half of the island, out of the volcano's danger zone. But on August 21 thousands of people were still in Plymouth when an eruption of steam and ash blackened the sky over the capital for 25 minutes.

SPECIFICATIONS

MONTSERRAT, 1997
Deaths: 19
Height of ash cloud: 30,000 feet (9,000 m)
Area buried: 0.8 square miles (2 sq km)
Speed of pyroclastic flow: 150 mph (240 km/h)

SPECIFICATIONS

MONTSERRAT, 2006
Height of gas cloud: 55,000 feet (17,000 m)
Rock erupted: 117 million cubic yards (90 million cu m)
Deaths: none
Injuries: none
Deepest ash in inhabited areas: 1.2 inches (3 cm)

> "It's the first thing you see when you wake up and the last thing you see when you go to bed. It tears at your soul."
>
> —A FARMER EVACUATED FROM HER HOME AND FORCED TO LIVE IN A SHELTER FOR TWO YEARS, ON HER VIEW OF SOUFRIÈRE HILLS

Left: Lava glows on the slopes of Soufrière Hills in 2002. The next year, the volcano's lava dome would disintegrate—the largest collapse of an active dome ever recorded—sending 275 million cubic yards (210 million cu. m) of rock careening downhill.

Below: Pyroclastic flows from Soufrière Hills course down the White River into the Caribbean Sea.

Minimal Losses

Fortunately, no one was killed, and as the volcano calmed to emit only hisses and grunts, authorities allowed refugees to return to the south of the island. Their time at home was short-lived. In early April 1996, the volcano began a continuous bout of ash eruptions of 30,000 feet (9,000 m) and blistering pyroclastic flows. The southerners were herded north again, to live indefinitely among the cots and sleeping bags that crowded nearly every church and school in the safe zone.

Unpleasant as life in the shelters proved—villagers slept 30 to a tent on cricket fields, and overburdened latrines fouled the air—the evacuations averted a tragedy. When Soufrière Hills deluged the south of Montserrat in 1997 it demolished houses, destroyed the airport, and buried the capital under tons of dust and rubble. But because of the evacuation, casualties were remarkably low: 19 people died, and 40 more survivors were pulled from the rubble.

Soufrière Hills continues to erupt. In 2003 it sent 275 million cubic yards (210 million cu. m) of rock hurtling downslope. Fortunately, scientists had been able to predict its direction and clear the area. In 2006 it exploded again.

Some two-thirds of Montserrat's residents have fled since 1995. For those who remain, Soufrière Hills's rages are now a way of life. The Montserrat Volcano Observatory monitors the volcano constantly, and children know to stop playing and run north when the alert sirens wail.

Mount St. Helens

A thick plume of smoke spews from the crater of Mount St. Helens on May 18, 1980. The column rose to 80,000 feet (24,400 m) within 15 minutes, and the ash cloud circled the globe over the next two weeks.

David Johnston had pulled Saturday-night duty at the Coldwater observation post, 5 miles (8 km) from Mount St. Helens in southwest Washington. The night of May 17, 1980, had been quiet, and when Sunday morning dawned, clear and sunny, the volcanologist radioed his data to the temporary U.S. Geological Survey base in Vancouver, Washington. The volcano had not changed much since the previous month, so it appeared there was no cause for alarm. But just after 8:30 AM, Johnston's voice blared over the radio link. "Vancouver, Vancouver,

SPECIFICATIONS

MOUNT ST. HELENS, 1980
Deaths: 57
Landslide area: 23 square miles (60 sq km)
Landslide volume: 0.67 cubic miles (2.8 cu km)
Maximum depth of landslide deposit:
  600 feet (180 m)
Landslide speed: 70 to 150 mph
  (110 to 240 km/h)
Blast area: 230 square miles (600 sq km)
Volume of blast deposit: 250 million cubic
  yards (190 million cu m)
Blast velocity: at least 300 mph
  (480 km/h)
Maximum blast temperature: 660°F (350°C)
Energy released by lateral blast: equal to
  24 megatons of TNT
Mudslide speed: about 10 to 25 mph
  (15 to 30 km/h); more than 50 mph
  (80 km/h) on steep flanks of volcano
Damages from mudslide: 27 bridges, nearly
  200 homes
Pyroclastic flow area covered: 6 square miles
  (15 sq km)
Pyroclastic flow volume and depth:
  155 million cubic yards (188 million
  cu m); multiple flows 3 to 30 feet
  (1–9 m) thick
Pyroclastic flow speed: estimated at 50 to
  80 mph (80–130 km/h)
Pyroclastic flow temperature: at least 1,300°F
  (700°C)
Ashfall volume: 0.26 cubic miles
  (1.1 cu km)
Area covered by ashfall: 22,000 square miles
  (57,000 sq km)

this is it!" he shouted. Seconds later, the crown of Mount St. Helens blew off with the force of 500 atomic bombs. In the next nine hours, hundreds of square miles of land would be decimated, primeval forests and northwestern towns would be buried under drifts of snowy ash, and scores would die. Among them was Johnston, whose body was never found.

Ring of Fire

The mountain had given some warning of the forces building up beneath its wooded slopes. Along with the other active volcanoes in the Cascade mountain range and in Alaska, Mount St. Helens lies over what is called the Ring of Fire, a chain of volcanoes and earthquake hot spots that circles the Pacific where tectonic plates rub together. The viscous, silica-rich magma boiling underneath Washington moves only under intense pressure, so Mount St. Helens does not erupt very often. But when it does, it is violent. Few witnesses had seen the last outburst in 1857, when the state was still mostly wilderness. After 123 years of sleep, the volcano stirred again on March 20, 1980. Several small earthquakes shook the slopes that day, followed by 10,000 more over the next two months. Blasts of steam opened a 1,300-foot (400 m) gash in the summit ice cap, and oozing lava had formed a 450-foot (140 m) bulge on the mountain's northern flank.

As molten rock leaked into the volcano's cavity from the Earth's inner layers, it heated groundwater, fueling the steam eruptions. The mounting pressure wedged the mountain apart from within by 5 feet (1.5 m) per day—hence the tremors—until the rock face finally gave way. At 8:32 AM on May 18, a magnitude 5.1 earthquake a mile below Mount St. Helens dislodged the swollen north flank, setting off a chain of events that rained destruction for hundred of miles.

Within about 10 seconds of the earthquake, both the bulge and the summit of Mount St. Helens were tumbling downslope at up to 150 miles per hour (240 km/h) in the largest landslide in recorded history. It buried 23 square miles (60 sq. km) under as much as 500 feet (150 m) of pebbles, boulders, ice, silt, and sand. Worse, though, the collapse of the mountain-side had an effect akin to unscrewing the cap from a shaken-up bottle of soda, but on a monumental scale. With the pressure suddenly released, the compressed gases inside the volcano exploded outward. The spray of ash, rock, steam, and poisonous, 600°F

"Keep Washington Green" reads the slogan on this Weyerhauser Company employee bus buried by the mudflow near the North Fork Toutle River (the bus was unoccupied when it was hit). As falling ash mixed with Mount St. Helens's melting snowpack, an avalanche of mud destroyed more than hundreds of miles of roadways and some 200 homes.

"the goldangest noise, like someone upending a bunch of barrels down the road. There was a roar, like a jet plane approaching, and a lot of snapping and popping. Those were the trees. We got out fast."

Mudslide

Like a cog in the volcano's machinery, the blast drove a column of ash and smoke 15 miles (25 km) into the air within 15 minutes. The column continued spewing a gigantic mushroom cloud for nine more hours, and as ash rained onto the volcano's slopes, its heat melted the glacial ice and snow. Trickles of slush soon joined into mudslides. As they barreled downhill at 80 miles per hour (130 km/h),

(300°C) volcanic gas flattened 230 square miles (600 sq. km) of timberland in fewer than five minutes. Within 6 miles (10 km) of the volcano, not a tree remained standing; farther out, where the blast had slowed to less than 300 miles per hour (480 km/h), charred trees leaned and some snapped like twigs. A logger at home near the north fork of the Toutle River heard the muddy torrents gathered rocks and boulders, clogging the Columbia, Cowlitz, and Toutle rivers with 20 to 30 feet (6–9 m) of sediment and stranding upstream ships. The avalanche battered some 200 houses and 27 bridges; a 1,300°F (700°C) pyroclastic cloud also dumped 155 million cubic yards (188 million cu. m) of pumice and ash over 6 square miles (15 sq. km) of Washington.

The eruption began to taper off by later afternoon and had stopped by the next morning. Although military helicopters rescued more than 100 people from the embers and debris, 57 died from burns or asphyxiation. Meanwhile, the volcano had unloaded millions of tons of cinder over 22,000 square miles (57,000 sq. km). The ash cloud would circle the Earth in two weeks before dissipating into the stratosphere. Southwest Washington lay under up to 10 inches (25 cm) of gray powder that fouled engines, water, and washing machines and transformed once-verdant hillsides and towns into a desolate moonscape.

Steam, carbon dioxide, and other gases escape from vents in the Kilauea volcano on the island of Hawaii. One of the most active volcanoes on Earth, Kilauea released 1,000 to 2,000 metric tons of sulfur dioxide into the atmosphere each day between 1986 and 2000.

ONGOING ERUPTIONS

In the past 25 years, at least 189 houses in a single district in Hawaii have been swallowed by lava from one of the big island's five active volcanoes. Sixty thousand more lots lie in the lava's probable path, but houses still sell like hotcakes. One homeowner explained the appeal: "There is an element of danger. But that makes life rich."

With any luck, Hawaiians can be as resourceful as the residents of another island considerably farther north. When the Eldfell volcano in Iceland erupted in 1973, lava flows threatened the fishing port of Vestmannaeyjar. The villagers decided to fight back. Using 19 miles (31 km) of pipe and 43 pumps, they sprayed 8 million cubic yards (6 million cu. m) of seawater at the advancing lava, crystallizing the molten rock into a dam that protected the town. Once the eruption ended, the villagers blasted away the hardened lava and rebuilt their damaged buildings.

Mount St. Helens before (left) and after (right) the 1980 eruption. The lateral blast and debris avalanche disgorged rock from the mountain, lopping off 1,314 feet (400 m) from the snowy peak. In its place gaped a crater 2,050 feet (625 m) deep and 1.7 miles (2.7 km) long.

"The Moon looks like a golf course compared to what's up there," President Jimmy Carter told reporters after a helicopter trip over the mountain. A Portland journalist added: "The living are not welcome here. The ground rejects you, trying to suck you into foot-deep mud. Chill winds knife into your spine. Ash floats in the air, killing your sense of smell. Every instinct, every emotion warns you to go away. I felt like we were trespassing, like we didn't have nature's permission to visit its ashen graves."

Among the dead were 7,000 deer, elk, and bears, 12 million salmon fingerlings, and $422 million worth of timber and crops in Washington, Idaho, and Montana. But the earth proved resilient even beneath this alien veil. The slightly acidic ash neutralized the area's alkaline soil and sealed in water, helping the region to turn in a bumper crop of wheat, hops, and apples. Within months, green sprouts were poking through the gray, and the ash bore the prints of returning deer. Humans, too, began to rebuild. Logging companies salvaged more than a quarter of the downed timber, and the cleanup operation provided so many jobs that it even drew newcomers. And as devastating as the eruption was, it brought a new boon to the area: tourism.

While the volcano continues to spout steam and ash, sightseers have flocked to photograph the reshaped Mount St. Helens, its once-symmetrical 9,677-foot (2,950 m) summit shorn to a lopsided, 8,636-foot (2,632 m) crater. By bringing money to the ravaged area, tourists helped with the cleanup. Vendors sold T-shirts and commemorative pens, but among the most popular items was "Genuine Mount St. Helens Volcanic Ash," at $1.98 per bag.

Mount Pinatubo, Philippines

Before 1991 no one but the Aeta people of the Philippines took much notice of Mount Pinatubo. The 4,900-foot (1,500 m) peak, which had not erupted for 450 years, had not even made the Smithsonian's registry of world volcanoes prior to 1981. The seminomadic Aeta lived on its gentle, wooded slopes. They fished from its rivers, hunted in its forests, and planted crops in its soil. The Aeta were aware that nature could be unpredictable, but little could have prepared them for the protracted, voluminous eruption that enveloped their home.

Earthquakes and Eruptions

Pinatubo, like Mount St. Helens, sits over the Ring of Fire, where heat from the Earth's interior and friction from grinding tectonic plates melt rock into volcanic magma. On July 16, 1980, a magnitude 7.8 earthquake struck Luzon, compressing the crust under the island. Other than a brief burst of extra steam, Pinatubo seemed to remain asleep for 11 more years. Magma rising from deep under the volcano continued to trigger small earthquakes, but on April 2, 1991, a stream of steam and ash jetted 2,600 feet (800 m) into the air. For the next two months, the volcano experienced 26 to 178 earthquakes a day.

On June 9 an explosion announced the world's largest eruption in 80 years.

For six days ash columns as high as 20 miles (30 km) blazed cascades of gas and pumice, and deafening blasts followed, building to the climax June 15. That day a new upwelling of magma caused 19 separate eruptions and 150 earthquakes per hour, sending ash 22 miles (35 km) into the air and raining more than 1 cubic mile (4 cu. km) of pumice chunks and searing cinder as far away as the Indian Ocean.

Once the mountain quieted on June 16, ash blanketed 1,500 square miles (4,000 sq. km), and pyroclastic clouds had flattened towns and cropland 10 miles (16 km) from the summit. More than 350 people died in the eruption, most of them when their roofs collapsed under the weight of ash—but the worst

> "When a nice little hill covered with lush vegetation finally wakes up,
> it's going to cause a lot of damage."
>
> —SMITHSONIAN VOLCANOLOGIST TOM SIMKIN

Left: In what almost looks like a negative image, trees and homes whitened by ash from Pinatubo stand against a black sky. Although more than 300 people died in the eruption, Philippine and American military authorities had evacuated another 78,000 from the area, thanks to warnings from scientists.

Opposite page: A cloud of smoke stretches into the air above Mount Pinatubo in June 1991. Ash and rock deposits buried an area of about 1,544 square miles (4,000 sq. km), killing crops and demolishing roofs.

was yet to come. A typhoon hit Luzon on June 15, mixing with the volcanic deposits to form raging torrents of mud. By fall more than 200 volcanic mudslides—some at temperatures of 160°F (70°C)—rushed down Pinatubo's slopes. The area often suffered five mudslides a day. Within months the mudslides did more damage than the eruption had. As they poured 30 feet (9 m) of cementlike wet ash over roads and bridges, 300,000 acres (1,200 sq. km) of land, and 29 towns, more than 300 people died and 100,000 were made homeless.

Stark as the numbers seem, they could have been much higher. Scientists were able to predict both the eruption and the mudslides, and the government evacuated people from Pinatubo's slopes, saving lives and up to $1 billion in property. Among the evacuees were 35,000 Aeta, who were crowded in evacuation camps, unable to resettle for years—some were never able to return to their original homelands.

UNZEN, JAPAN, 1792

A month after Mount Unzen, a volcano east of Nagasaki on the Japanese island of Kyushu, stopped spurting molten rock in 1792, one of its lava domes collapsed. A massive landslide—probably a pyroclastic flow—barreled through Shimabara city, killing thousands of people, and fell into a shallow inland sea.

Abetted by ground tremors, the landslide generated a tsunami that swept the neighboring coastlines, drowning thousands of people and demolishing 3,000 houses. Combined, the avalanche and tsunami killed 15,000, the deadliest volcanic disaster ever in a country with more than 75 active volcanoes.

Nevado del Ruiz, Colombia

When Nevado del Ruiz, which southwestern Colombians call their "Sleeping Lion," erupted on November 13, 1985, the mayor of Armero turned on his ham radio. In a valley about 30 miles (50 km) from the summit, Armero was well out of range of the millions of tons of ash the long-dormant volcano now spat into the air. Mayor Ramón Antonio Rodríguez was the first to report the event to the wider world. He was placidly describing the unfolding action to a distant fellow radio operator when his tone abruptly shifted. "Wait a minute," he shouted. "I think the town is getting flooded." They were his last words.

The Fertile Land

Although they did not realize it, the residents of the peaceful, prosperous agricultural center at Armero owed their prosperity to Ruiz's previous two eruptions. In 1595 and again in 1845, pyroclastic clouds set off mudslides that killed hundreds of people but also spread 250 million tons of lime over the valleys. Through the years, as the mountain fell into more than a century of slumber, the deposits decomposed into a layer of rich topsoil 25 feet (8 m) thick. In Armero memories faded of the bodies struck down on that very spot, and by the 1980s the city boasted upward of 30,000 residents.

Beneath the fertile ground, though, the Earth was churning. Magma melting off the Pacific plate as it bent beneath the South American landmass was slowly bubbling to Ruiz's surface. In November 1984 the mountain began to tremble and spurt, producing steam and earthquakes into the following summer. Around that time, a team from the Colombian Institute of Geoscience trekked to the 17,453-foot (5,321 m) summit, which was cloaked in sulfurous clouds. Scientists in July 1985 set up the first seismographs to measure the volcano. Two months later, on September 11, Ruiz spouted a seven-hour shower of ash. That month, volcanologists recommended that the Colombian government evacuate the towns around the

"Suddenly, out of the canyon wherein the Lagunilla River flows, an enormous and strange torrent of thick mud became dislodged at tremendous velocity."

—HISTORIAN RAFAEL GÓMEZ PICÓN ON THE FEBRUARY 1845 ERUPTION

volcano, even drawing a map of the specific communities mudslides might hit.

The key word was "might." The scientists could not predict exactly when—or, for certain, if—Ruiz would explode. It might steam and rumble for months or years before erupting, or it might fall dormant again without an explosion. Rather than needlessly hazard a billion-dollar disruption to the economy by evacuating thousands of citizens, the departmental governor assured the public that "there are no immediate risks."

Complacency

Even as they watched the sulfur plume climb higher and higher, the villagers at the base of Nevado del Ruiz accepted the reassurance. "They were saying, 'That is not going to happen,'" remembered Marta Calvache, head of the scientific team, of her attempt to warn the townspeople. "'It doesn't happen for more than 100 years. Why is it going to happen now?'" An Armero priest explained the prevailing attitude: "We knew the danger was there. But we just cheerfully got accustomed to it." The Colombian government did finally authorize a mudslide-drainage canal and a disaster plan, but neither project got a chance to start. As a deputy chief with the U.S. Geological Survey lamented, "The volcano erupted too soon."

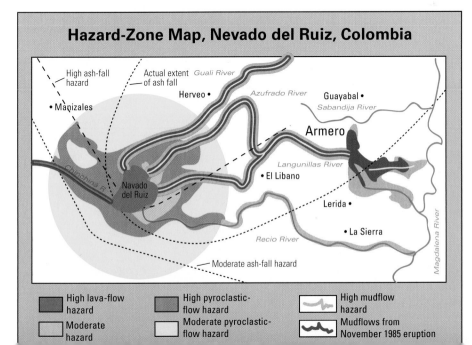

Hazard-Zone Map, Nevado del Ruiz, Colombia

High ash-fall hazard
Actual extent of ash fall *Guali River*
Herveo •
Azufrado River
Guayabal •
Sabandija River
• Manizales
Armero
Chinchiná R.
Navado del Ruiz
Langunillas River
• El Libano
Lerida •
• La Sierra
Recio River
Moderate ash-fall hazard
Magdalena River

High lava-flow hazard
Moderate hazard
High pyroclastic-flow hazard
Moderate pyroclastic-flow hazard
High mudflow hazard
Mudflows from November 1985 eruption

A map showing likely paths for lava, mudslides, and pyroclastic flows in future Ruiz eruptions. Scientists had prepared such a map prior to the 1985 event, but Colombian officials declined to evacuate the threatened towns.

Background: Nevado del Ruiz as it looks today. The glaciers and snow at its peak turned deadly during the 1985 eruption, when they melted and mixed with searing ash to create mudslides that were over 100 feet thick.

Rivers of Mud

At 3:05 PM November 13, Nevado del Ruiz exploded powerfully enough that the government ordered the evacuation of nearby towns. But by 7:00 that evening, the volcano seemed to have calmed down, and the evacuation was called off. Meanwhile, a fierce rainstorm darkened the sky and blocked the view of the summit. Then, at 9:08 PM, just as residents were getting in bed, came a detonation so loud a civil defense worker 150 miles (240 km) away "thought it might be a terrorist bombing in our neighborhood." Turbulent, searing pyroclastic clouds spilled 26-foot-deep (8 m) mounds of ash on the summit, and hot pumice fell with the rain northeast of the mountain.

All told, the two eruptions ejected 26 million cubic yards (20 million cu. m) of fiery debris: a moderate showing, as far as eruptions go. But when the glowing ash and shards of rock landed on Ruiz's glacier, they melted some 10 percent of the mountain's ice and snow. Soon scalding torrents of water, pumice, and ash were surging down the slopes, sucking up loose debris and water until they were viscous walls of mud up to 50 feet (15 m) high and 132 feet (40 m) wide. Charging down all six of the mountain's riverbeds at 30 miles per hour (50 km/h), the lahars made for the towns downstream.

"First there were earth tremors," remembered a mother of two in Armero. "The air suddenly seemed heavy. It smelled of sulfur. Then there was a horrible rumbling that seemed to come from deep inside the earth." Two and a half hours after the eruption, the muddy wave "rolled into town with a moaning sound, like some sort of monster. . . . Houses below us started cracking under the advance of the river of mud. It seemed like the end of the world." Within minutes Armero was buried under 7 to 15 feet (2 to 5 m) of sludge, punctured here and there by roof gables, pools of blood, and jutting human limbs. Eighty percent of the town's houses had been swallowed, and those who had been unable to climb trees or scale rooftops before the onslaught died. Armero lost 23,000 people, three-quarters of its population.

Three other towns within 60 miles (100 km) of Ruiz endured similar fates, although Armero suffered the worst. With an almost immediate donation of $50 million from governments and charities around the world, rescue workers fought washed-out roads, downpours, and lingering ashfall to pry survivors encased and choking in mud. One 13-year-old girl, buried up to her neck, survived for 60 hours while rescue workers tried to free her.

She died before they succeeded; when her body was finally unearthed, it was still tight in the grip of her aunt, who had suffocated days earlier.

These two victims were among more than 25,000 to die as a result of the eruption. Five thousand more were injured, and 8,000 lost their homes. Angry Colombians blamed the government, which had failed to evacuate the threatened towns. Scientists, distraught that they had not prevented the disaster, resolved to be better prepared in the future. Months after Ruiz erupted, the U.S. Geological Survey and the Office of Foreign Disaster Assistance established a traveling coterie of volcanologists and state-of-the-art portable monitoring equipment, which could be dispatched at a moment's notice to an awakening volcano. Their assistance to local forecasters and governments has already saved property and lives, most notably at Mount Pinatubo in 1991.

The town of Armero, Colombia, lies buried under 15 feet (4.5 m) of mud. The town lost more than 20,000 citizens in minutes as mud and boulders swept away or subsumed 5,000 homes.

FERTILE ASH

As destructive as eruptions are, over decades and centuries their ash can prove extremely beneficial. Some of the planet's most fertile soil—from the lush jungles of Hawaii and Indonesia to the valleys that have supported civilization in Greece and Italy since ancient times—formed from the breakdown of volcanic ash.

As the ash weathers, it releases iron, magnesium, and potassium, which nourish vegetation. The ash cover also prevents moisture from evaporating out of the ground. With heavy enough rain, plants can begin to peek through the cinders in less than a year after a massive eruption.

CHAPTER 8

TSUNAMIS

IN JAPANESE, TSUNAMI MEANS "HARBOR WAVE."
But the literal translation fails to convey the sheer brutality
of the real thing. In the West tsunamis used to be called tidal
waves, although they have nothing to do with the tides. They
well up when a large enough force—an earthquake, landslide,
volcanic flow, or meteor—disturbs the ocean. Like ripples on a
pond, the swells spread at jetliner speed over an ever-expanding
area from their source. They travel in stealth over the open
ocean, transforming into towering, lethal walls of water when
they get to shallow coastal areas.

   To the people on land, the sea betrays few hints of a
tsunami's imminent metamorphosis. The ocean may bubble
as though boiling, or it might recede from the beach. Curious
bystanders often rush in for a closer look, only to be lured
into a collection of humankind's worst fears. Tsunamis kill by
drowning, by crushing, by burying, and by impaling. On land,
they can move faster than a cheetah, and to be swept up in one
of their surges is to become its hapless missile. It is impossible
to swim out of this wave; the only hope is to grab a tree or a
lamppost, if the water has not already snapped it off. Anyone
who survives the impact of the wave will likely be killed when it
throws them into a wall or a hill, or to the ground.

Left: The aftermath in Seward, Alaska, of the tsunami that ripped down
the West Coast in March 1964. Splintered logs, disembodied rooftops,
and transplanted appliances testify to tsunamis' destructive power. The
sharp snowline on the hillside marks the height of the highest wave;
the rushing water washed the snow from the slopes below that point.
Inset: A beachside sign marks a tsunami hazard zone. Tsunamis develop
quickly, often before agencies can detect them and alert the public. For
that reason, it is important for oceanside residents and beachgoers to be
familiar with the warning signs and evacuation routes.

Right: Wooden shrapnel litters the beach at Lebak, on the Philippine island of Mindanao, after a tsunami in the Moro Gulf on August 16, 1976. Like many tsunamis, this one was caused by an undersea earthquake. High waves flooded hundreds of miles of shoreline and killed 8,000 people.

Opposite page: A meteor hurtles toward Earth in this disquieting photomontage. Large meteors may have crashed into the ocean within the past 5,000 years; such an event could generate a catastrophic tsunami.

PROBLEMS WITH PREDICTION

While common in the Pacific, tsunamis are a once-a-century event in the Indian Ocean. This is one reason that no government in the region had considered it worth the investment to develop a tsunami warning system. The seafloor earthquake that caused the 2004 tsunami registered on seismometers in Hawaii. Large quakes do not always cause tsunamis, but NOAA scientists issued an alert just in case.

Once the tsunami struck, it traveled faster than communications, especially given that no dedicated alert network was in place. Worse yet, the public, never having seen a tsunami, failed to recognize the signs when they saw them, and flocked to the beach to watch the ocean recede.

Since the 2004 disaster scientists and governments have been working to establish a tsunami-detection system and to educate the public on the warning signs and emergency procedures.

Obviously, the best defense is to head for higher ground before the wave hits. But outrunning a tsunami is no easy feat, especially because it strikes so suddenly. Predicting whether an earthquake or landslide will trigger a tsunami is tricky and must be done quickly for public alerts to do any good. In 1993, 104-foot (32 m) waves hit Japan four minutes after the earthquake that caused them. The government warnings were delivered about a minute later.

As scientists continue to improve their understanding of these disasters, public-education programs have taught residents of tsunami-prone areas to recognize the red flags on their own. The Japanese, who are tsunami veterans, know to run for the hills or even climb a tree when the ocean froths. That sort of knowledge could have saved hundreds of thousands of lives on the Indian Ocean in December 2004.

PREHISTORIC METEORS

We know earthquakes and landslides can cause tsunamis, but what would happen if a large meteor crashed into the ocean? Judging from the historical evidence, the resulting mega-tsunami could trigger biblical-caliber floods and bury coasts in sediment. As recently as 4,800 years ago, some scientists believe, a meteor plunged into the Indian Ocean, throwing up a wave 600 feet (180 m) high. Researchers have found a crater 18 miles (30 km) wide in the ocean floor; in the depression, fossils are fused with the metals usually found at cosmic impact sites. The location and timing fit with sediments on adjacent coasts and the preponderance of flood myths in the region.

"We're not talking about any tsunami you've ever seen," Ted Bryant, an Australian geomorphologist, told the *New York Times*. "Aceh was a dimple. No tsunami in the modern world could have made these features. End-of-the-world movies do not capture the size of these waves." Geologists have also found deposits in Texas that suggest another comet-incited tsunami around the end of the Cretaceous period, 65 million years ago.

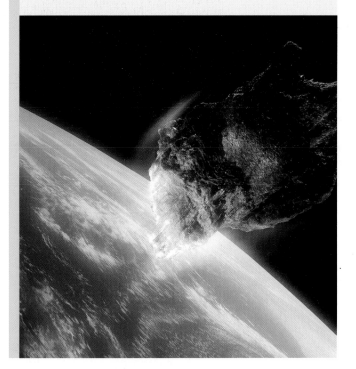

Sumatra, 2004

Fishermen far out on the water would have felt only a bump, a wave a foot or two high rolling under their hulls. Early-morning beachcombers noticed something more unusual, and they crowded the shoreline to watch. The sea was draining away, baring yards of never-before-seen ocean floor. Fish writhed on the sand, and boats ran aground in the new shallows. Tourists in Thailand grabbed their cameras; Sri Lankans snatched up the fish for dinner. "People were saying it was something to do with the full moon," a Finnish vacationer in Thailand remembered. There were no sirens, no radio or television alerts, no warnings of what loomed offshore. "I heard this strange thunderous sound from somewhere," recalled a fisherman from the Indonesian island of Sumatra. "A sound I'd never heard before. I thought it was the sound of bombs." He turned around, and a 50-foot (15 m) wall of water crashed over his head. It carried him 2 miles (3 km); he survived by grabbing hold of a coconut tree. "It felt like doomsday," he said.

Hour by hour, advancing west with the morning sun, the same tragedy repeated itself along the coasts of the Indian Ocean. On December 26, 2004, the most destructive tsunami in history rippled

A valley near Phuket, Thailand, continues to dry out after being completely engulfed during the December 2004 tsunami. Waves towered 10 to 15 feet (3 to 5 m) at the nation's shore.

SPECIFICATIONS

SUMATRA, 2004
Earthquake magnitude: 9.1 to 9.3
Maximum wave height: 160 feet (50 m)
Wave speed in open water: 500 mph (800 km/h)
Deaths: more than 200,000
Homeless: 1.8 million
Damages: $10 billion

"It lifted up 11 yards and paused, almost like it was surveying us below it. And then it fell. It consumed one house after another, like paper boxes."

—Baalaramanan, a fisherman in Akkarapettai, India

across a quarter of the globe, killing hundreds of thousands of people in 13 countries.

The Cause

The devastation all stemmed from a single, 750-mile (1,200 km) rift in the ocean floor. At 7:58 local time the morning after Christmas Day, a magnitude 9.1 to 9.3 earthquake 150 miles (240 km) off the northern coast of Sumatra heaved up billions of tons of water. When the crest crashed back down, it split into two parallel surges, one flowing east and the other west. In the deep water of the open ocean, the swells were less than 2 feet (0.6 m) high, but as they bumped against the continental shelf, they piled up on themselves. The wave trough hit Sumatra 10 minutes after the quake, which is what caused the sea level to drop. As would happen again and again across the continent, people rushed to the beach to look. Then the tsunami reared up. Walls of water 30 to 60 feet high (9–20 m) slammed as far as 6 miles (10 km) inland, uprooting trees, pulver-

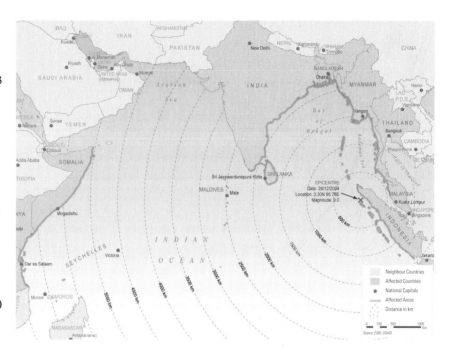

izing buildings, tossing cars like confetti. In Banda Aceh, on the northern tip of Sumatra, waves met from either side of the island. Within 10 minutes, one-third of the city's 320,000 residents were dead, dragged out to sea or crushed under tons of water.

Thailand was next. "How the hell anyone survived has got me licked," said an Australian vacationer in Phuket, which was struck an hour after the quake. "The second wave carried a car right toward me, but I was able to shift to one side and watch it shoot past. The worst part was, you could see the bodies going out in the water."

This United Nations map shows areas affected by the 2004 earthquake and tsunami. The epicenter of the earthquake was located off the west coast of northern Sumatra. The boundaries and names shown and the designations used on this map do not imply official endorsement or acceptance by the United Nations.

Sea of Despair

Traveling west at 450 miles per hour (720 km/h), the tsunami approached Sri Lanka and India at about 9 AM. "It was a sunny day," remembered one Sri Lankan, "but everything became really gray and dark. And everything lost its color. All I could see was a wall of water that took up about 80 to 85 percent of the horizon; the sky was blocked." Muddy surges spiked with vehicles, boats, and people wrapped around the island, destroying 43,000 buildings and plunging survivors—who clung to roofs or floated on pieces of debris—into snake-filled currents. In India, as many as 300 people from a seaside market were flushed 2 miles (3 km) inland, their bodies dumped by the waves among 5,000 other dead.

Seven hours and 3,000 miles (5,000 km) later, the tsunami still had enough power to kill hundreds of people in Somalia. The waves would circle the globe before dissipating, damaging the seaside in 18 countries, from Australia to South Africa. Having risen that morning over typical fishing villages and resort towns, the sun set on what looked like an atomic war zone. The same disorienting, dissonant scene played across thousands of miles of coastline: Upside-down cars and boats lay amid shards of brick and mud-blackened timber, puckering pages

Below: A row of houses crumples to the ground in Aceh, Sumatra. The tsunami left 1.8 million people homeless, 426,800 of them in Sumatra. A year later, 100,000 still had no permanent dwellings.

Opposite page: What remains of a Sumatran village lies flooded and strewn with debris. Just 150 miles (240 km) from the tsunami's origin, Sumatra was hardest hit by the punishing waves: More than 108,000 of the more than 200,000 dead were from Sumatra.

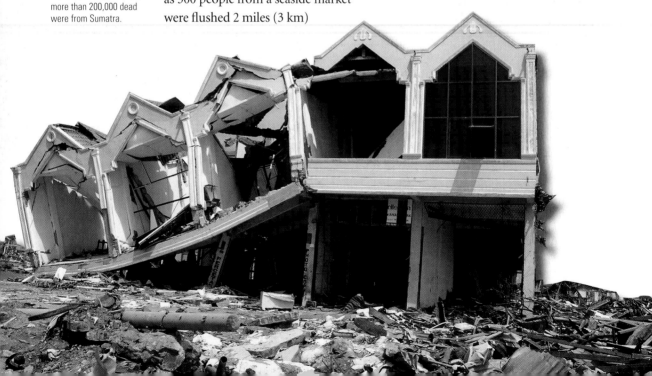

of notebook paper, in some places a child's shoe. And everywhere—popping up from lagoon bottoms, hanging in trees, lining the streets—were the corpses. More than 200,000 people died in the tsunami, almost half in Indonesia, another tenth in Sri Lanka.

In Thailand many of the dead were European tourists on their winter holidays, but elsewhere the sea killed the subsistence farmers and fishermen who squeezed out a living at its edge. As the smell of rotting flesh in the tropical sun grew intolerable in the next days, hollow-eyed parents and children said goodbye to their loved ones over mass graves and funeral pyres. One-third of the dead were children, a reflection of both the high birthrate in Southeast Asia and the youngest victims' inability to outrun or outclimb the waves. The tsunami made orphans of tens of thousands more, many of whom watched their parents drown.

THE EARTHQUAKE EFFECT

It was the second- or third-largest shock ever recorded, more powerful than every earthquake from the five previous years combined. The temblor that triggered the 2004 tsunami occurred below the Indian Ocean northwest of Sumatra, where the Indian, Australian, and Eurasian plates collide. As the Indian plate shoves north into Asia at 0.8 inches (20 mm) a year, it slips under the sliver of the Earth's crust that holds Burma. At 7:58 AM on December 26, the plates suddenly shifted about 65 feet (19.8 m) in four minutes, creating a rupture more than 600 miles (nearly 1,000 km) long.

During the quake, the ocean floor on the western side of the fault rose 15 feet (5 m), while the seafloor east of the rupture dropped 7 feet (2 m). The water above mirrored the undulations below: A huge column of water was boosted up west of the fault, while the eastern side dropped. Just like kicking your feet underwater in a pool, the seafloor motion created a wave, but this one lethal, with the energy of 20,000 atomic bombs.

Outpouring of Support

Given the sheer vastness of the tsunami's destruction, the relief effort, which turned out to be the largest in history, was a logistical quagmire. The tsunami had done $10 billion in damages in a region that was in many places already both impoverished and war-torn. Despite $13 billion in international aid, relief workers had trouble reaching areas isolated by washed-out roads. Yet even in overcrowded camps, few survivors succumbed to disease, starvation, or thirst, thanks to the vigilance of emergency responders and public-health workers. Tensions between separatists in Sumatra and the Indonesian government relaxed in the aftermath, although disagreements over the disbursal of aid may have only deepened the rift between Sri Lankan authorities and the northern rebels.

Right: A bulletin board in Phuket, Thailand, shows unidentified victims of the tsunami. More than 5,000 people were killed in Thailand, and 3,100 were missing along the coast. Many were European vacationers who had come on their Christmas holiday to enjoy the area beaches.

Below: Two men take a break from the search for victims in Phuket, Thailand. Death was everywhere along the shores of the Indian Ocean, and corpses quickly began to decay in the tropical heat.

The tsunami left 1.8 million homeless, and a year later more than 100,000 Indonesians still lived in camps or tents. Only a tenth of the 1,900 miles (3,000 km) of blocked roads had been repaired. A shortage of labor and timber slowed rebuilding from Thailand to India, although the effort outpaced that following many past calamities. For many, though, a new home could never replace what they had lost. One 25-year-old from southern India buried 11 members of his family the week after the tsunami. "Since my childhood, I've known nothing more closely than the sea," he said. "Now I hate it."

Satellite images of Gleebruk, a small town in Indonesia's Aceh province, before (left) and after (right) the 2004 tsunami. The wooded hills were beyond the reach of the waves, but buildings, trees, and beaches were not.

TILLY SMITH

Ten-year-old British schoolgirl Tilly Smith was strolling on the beach on vacation with her parents and younger sister in Phuket, Thailand, the morning of December 26, 2004, when the ocean began acting strange. "The sea was all frothy like on the top of a beer," Tilly recalled. "It was bubbling." Then the tide went out, and Tilly got scared. Her geography teacher had discussed just this phenomenon two weeks earlier, in a class on tsunamis. "I was hysterical," she said later. "I was screaming . . . 'Seriously, there is definitely going to be a tsunami!'"

Her parents believed her. They persuaded other tourists to evacuate the area, and Tilly's father notified a security guard. Thanks to Tilly, when the tsunami hit, not a single person died on that beach.

Hilo, Hawaii, 1946

Deep beneath the dark, icy waters of the North Pacific, a shudder rippled through the seafloor. At 3:29 AM on April 1, 1946, from 15 miles (25 km) below the ocean off the Aleutian Islands, a magnitude 7.8 earthquake sent seismographs scribbling. Offshore tremors are common along the faults that trace Alaska's south coast, but they rarely cause much harm. This one would set off a tsunami that toppled buildings as far away as Antarctica.

The earthquake levered up a huge block of the seafloor. That vertical movement, like a giant rising oar, welled up an equally large wave that instantly fanned out to find land. Forty-eight minutes later, a 135-foot (40 m) surge engulfed the U.S. Coast Guard's six-year-old, five-story lighthouse on Unimak Island, Alaska. Guardsmen from a nearby bunkhouse ran into the night in their underwear to find the steel-reinforced beacon completely destroyed and its five crew members killed. The survivors quickly sent out an SOS, which was taken on the other end for an April Fools' Day joke. "They ignored us," one of the guardsmen remembered.

Total Disbelief

Skeptics would continue to doubt the existence of the monster wave as it tore its way south down the west coast of North America. Moving at 500 miles per hour (800 km/h), the tsunami washed away boats and homes in Alaska, splintered docks in British Columbia, and gushed up to a quarter mile inland in California, where it took its sixth victim in 10-foot (3 m) waves at Santa Cruz.

More than 2,000 miles (3,200 km) from its origin, the tsunami raced toward Hawaii. The islands had only recently recovered from World War II. The barbed wire and blackout paint were finally gone, rations a thing of the past, families reunited. Now, with no warning of what was bearing down on them—tsunami alert systems did not yet exist—children got ready for school. Four and a half hours after the earthquake, the looming wave sucked the water from the shore. Children, fascinated by the sight of flopping fish and the bare seafloor, ran to look. "I watched the water just recede away," one survivor remembered, "like someone pulled the plug in a bathtub."

Another recalled his brother and friends yelling "Tidal wave!" "I said,

The 1946 tsunami traveled the more than 2,000 miles (3,200 km) from its origin in the Aleutians to Hawaii in just over four hours. The city of Hilo, Hawaii, suffered the worst.

"The wave flipped me over and carried me toward the lava rock wall. . . .
I recall telling myself, 'I'm going to hit headfirst into that rock wall and
I'm going to die.'"

—MASUO KINO, SURVIVOR ON THE ISLAND OF HAWAII

The Scotch Cap lighthouse on Unimak Island, Alaska, before (left) and after (right) the 1946 tsunami. A 135-foot (40 m) wave engulfed the structure, demolishing all but the foundation and part of the concrete seawall. All five occupants were killed.

'Baloney. This is April 1, you think you're going to—' But their faces were very white. I said, 'No, they're not kidding.'" All too soon, curious sightseers witnessed a terrifying sight: a 50-foot (15 m) wave rushing toward the shore at 490 miles per hour (790 km/h). Water spilled inland, throwing boxcars through buildings and leveling entire blocks. Hilo, on the island of Hawaii, got the worst of it. Eight waves wiped out its entire waterfront and drowned 98 people. Elsewhere in the Hawaiian Islands, 61 more people died and nearly a hundred homes were reduced to rubble. Dead fish, smashed boats, and fallen coconuts littered the beach.

The tsunami managed to damage boats in Chile, kill two people in the Marquesas Islands, and demolish an observation hut in Antarctica before dying out. The final death toll stood at 167, and damages topped $26 million in 1946 dollars. The idea that advance warning might have prevented some of those deaths inspired American scientists to establish a center in Hawaii to monitor the ocean and detect oncoming tsunamis.

ANCIENT EVIDENCE

Some 120,000 years ago a giant landslide from the slopes of Mauna Loa, a volcano on the island of Hawaii, crashed into the Pacific Ocean. The falling debris stirred up a tsunami that washed almost 4 miles (6 km) inland. Scientists have discovered deposits on the island—smashed coral and shells, shards of lava, coralline sand—in an area that seems to have been denuded of topsoil and vegetation. The scientists tested the deposits and estimated them to be 120,000 years old, which matched with the date of the last landslide on Mauna Loa's western slope.

Chile, 1960

The nation of Chile lies along an active fault zone on the Pacific Coast. In June 1960 Chile had been convulsing on and off for a month. The worst damage had come in May, when the strongest earthquake yet recorded hurled a swarm of towering waves across the Pacific.

The morning of May 21, a magnitude 7.5 earthquake hammered the coast of central Chile, leveling buildings in the city of Concepción. The next afternoon at 3:10, another, equally powerful quake struck. Moments later, with debris still falling, the shaking exploded into a seven-minute, magnitude 9.5 temblor that split the seafloor for 620 miles (1,000 km). The Nazca plate below the Pacific Ocean, which usually nudges under the South American plate at 3.3 inches (8.4 cm) per year, pitched some 60 feet (18 m) in one afternoon.

SPECIFICATIONS

CHILE, 1960
Earthquake magnitude: 9.5
Top wave height: at least 82 feet (25 m)
Tsunami speed in open ocean: more than 500 mph (800 km/h)
Deaths: 2,290 in Chile, 200 in Japan, 61 in Hilo, Hawaii
Damages: $550 million in Chile, $75 million in Hawaii ($23.5 million in Hilo), $50 million in Japan, $1 million on the West Coast of the U.S.

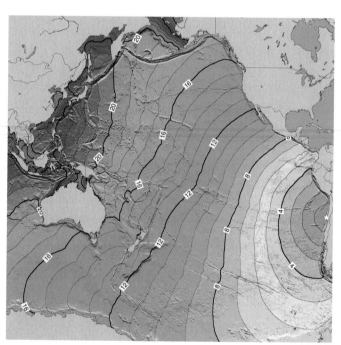

From Chile to Japan

On Isla Chiloé, just off Chile's south-central coast, terrified survivors crowded onto the water in small boats to avoid the collapsing debris. Then,

"As our eyes searched for the source of the ominous noise, a pale wall of tumbling
water, the broken crest of the third wave, was caught in the dim light
thrown across the water by the lights of Hilo."

Left: A house rests in a new location in Ancud, Chile, after a 50-foot (15 m) wave washed it from its foundation. The tsunami struck the town 50 minutes after a devastating earthquake.

Below: Hilo again bore the brunt of the tsunami in Hawaii in 1960. Fifteen hours after they ravaged Chile, the waves arrived in Hawaii, destroying Hilo's business district and several residential areas.

10 minutes after the earthquake, the ocean seemed to empty, pulling out more than 1,500 feet (450 m) from the shore. Moments later the inhabitants of Chiloé spied a 70-foot (20 m) wave poised over the tiny boats. The surf crashed more than a mile inland, sucking entire villages into the ocean and drenching parts of Chile in up to 13 feet (3.9 m) of water. One tree along the Rio Maullín supported eight survivors that night while the waters swirled around its trunk.

Barely rippling the open ocean, the tsunami made for Hawaii at 520 miles per hour (840 km/h). Hawaiian geologists had been anxiously monitoring the sea since the previous day's earthquakes and issued an official warning at 6:47 PM local time. In Hilo, on the island of Hawaii, the sirens sounded at 8:30 PM, but few residents realized it was an evacuation signal. Just after midnight, the claxon was replaced with a rumbling, then an unearthly crunching. "Suddenly I heard a shout, 'Big wave!'" remembered a survivor. "The streetlights around us exploded almost in the same instant. I looked up and saw a locally well-known fishing boat coming up over the Wailoa Bridge." Eight successive waves, the tallest 35 feet (10 m), tossed around boulders and tractors, bent parking meters like pipe cleaners, and crushed 537 buildings in Hilo. Although Maui and Oahu escaped with little damage, the tsunami flattened downtown Hilo, causing $23.5 million in damages and killing 61 people.

Ten thousand miles from Chile, 14-foot (4.3 m) waves drenched the east coast of Japan 22 hours after the earthquake. Two hundred people were killed and 5,000 homes destroyed in the 18-hour onslaught. Before dissipating two days later, the tsunami hit every ocean and thrashed beachfront structures from California to New Zealand. In all, the rushing water did more than $600 million in damages, most of it in Chile, where 2,290 people were killed by the earthquake and tsunami. Along with the rubble and the newly drowned near one Chilean village, caskets and crosses from the local cemetery had been washed several miles upriver. "The tsunami was so big," the villagers took to saying, "that it even took the dead from their graves."

Destruction on a street in Isla Chiloe. The island's inhabitants had rushed to their boats to escape the earthquake, only to be confronted 10 minutes later with giant tsunami waves. Two hundred people died on the island.

CRESCENT CITY, CALIFORNIA, 1964

Fittingly enough, North America's strongest-ever earthquake triggered the worst tsunami in the continental United States. After a magnitude 9.2 earthquake ruptured the floor of Prince William Sound near Alaska, tsunami waves surged down the West Coast. The swells killed 106 people in Alaska and 4 in Oregon before crashing ashore in Crescent City, just across the border in California.

Residents of the harbor town were used to flooding and went about their business as the first wave dumped a foot of water over the downtown. The next three waves, however, battered the little town with enough power to scatter 1,000 cars around 5 square miles (13 sq. km) of town. "It was like a violent explosion," wrote Peggy Coons and her husband, Roxey, the keepers for Crescent City's lighthouse. "A thunderous roar mingled with all the confusion. Everywhere we looked, buildings, cars, lumber, and boats shifted around like crazy. The whole beachfront moved, changing before our very eyes." In Crescent City alone the waves caused $350 million in damages (in 2005 dollars) and killed 11 people.

Japan Faces the Waves

The fishermen returning home from the open sea on the morning of June 16, 1896, thought they spied something unusual in the water. In Japan in the nineteenth century, it was customary for fishing boats to go out in the evening and return the following day. Even though June 15 was a holiday—the Boys Festival, a time for families to fete their young sons—the men of Honshu, Japan's largest island, had gone to work. But as they made for shore at sunup, they noticed something strange: houses floating on the breakers. Closer up, they began to make out

The Great Wave at Kanagawa, a woodblock print by the Japanese artist Katsushika Hokusai from the early 1830s. Japan has faced hundreds of tsunamis, and the Japanese have grown adept at identifying and escaping them.

SPECIFICATIONS

JAPAN, 1896
Earthquake magnitude: 7.2
Maximum tsunami wave height: 125 feet (38 m)
Reach inland: 100 miles (160 km)
Deaths: 27,122
Injured: 9,247
Houses destroyed: 10,617
Houses damaged: 2,456

large pieces of debris being tossed by the waves. But there was something else in the water, too. The boats had to make their way past innumerable corpses to reach the harbor.

"In some cases the victim looks as though it had been plunged in boiling water and almost every body shows purple spots as if it had been fiercely pelted with fragments of stone or iron."

—A REPORTER, ON TSUNAMI VICTIMS, 1896

Lethal waves have battered Japan probably 150 times since the earliest record, in 684 CE. But none of the revelers on the beach that warm summer evening thought they were in any danger.

A Celebration Turns Deadly

Along the coast of Sanriku, a province on the island of Honshu, every town was celebrating. They all felt the magnitude 7.2 earthquake that rumbled from the seafloor 120 miles (190 km) offshore at 7:32 PM, but in a country beset by 15 earthquakes a year, this was no reason to worry. Quakes that small do not usually start tsunamis, but this one, unfortunately, struck in shallow water and lasted up to 100 seconds. By the time the little earthquake finally stopped shaking, it had generated a huge tsunami.

People celebrating on the beach suddenly noticed the water receding. Then they heard a hiss, like oncoming rain. Most of them were killed instantly by waves towering as high as 125 feet (38 m). More than 27,000 people died along 300 miles (480 km) of coast, as the waves rushed 100 miles (160 km) inland. In most cases, officials found it simpler to calculate village death tolls by subtracting the number of survivors from the population rather than adding up all the dead.

A true-color satellite image of Japan in May 2003. Japan lies in the Ring of Fire, a region where tectonic plates collide and generate earthquakes, tsunamis, and volcanic eruptions.

While villagers, using fishing nets, pulled the dead from the ocean by the scores, donations poured in from around the world. The waves had washed away 10,617 houses and damaged another 2,456; every single coastal town in the Mino and Owari provinces had been annihilated. In the following weeks, diseases festered in remote villages that aid workers were unable to reach. Government coffers had been emptied the year before to finance the Sino-Japanese War, but with alms from private donors, the survivors eventually rebuilt, this time farther away from the shore.

Above: This map shows the location of Okushiri Island and the epicenter of the quake that caused the 1993 tsunami. The waves took as little as two minutes to reach the island.

Below: A beached fishing boat and a roof lie among debris on Okushiri Island on July 14, 1993. The tsunami flooded the island before warnings could get through.

Okushiri, 1993

By the early 1990s the Japanese had a warning system in place. Whenever an earthquake disturbed the nearby waters—which occurred, on average, at least once a month—the Japan Meteorological Agency calculated the danger and issued an alert within minutes. On the night of July 12, 1993, when a magnitude 7.8 quake struck 50 miles (80 km) off Okushiri Island in the Sea of Japan, the agency pinpointed the at-risk areas in five minutes. Unfortunately, however, the alerts did not make it to all their intended destinations. The tremor had downed utility lines across Okushiri and nearby Hokkaido, the northernmost of Japan's main islands, and in many towns the warnings crawled in by fax or not at all. But even in the

SPECIFICATIONS

OKUSHIRI, 1993
Earthquake magnitude: 7.8
Time after earthquake that tsunami hit Okushiri:
2 to 5 minutes
Maximum wave height: 104 feet (32 m)
Deaths: 230 total; more than 200 from tsunami
Damages: Japan, $66 million; Russia, $6 million
Houses destroyed: 427
Houses damaged or flooded: 885

areas they reached, the messages did little good. The quake struck at 10:17 PM, and hundred-foot waves swamped Okushiri at 10:21. By the time the agency bulletins came through, the island lay underwater.

The tsunami hit the little village of Monai, directly across from the epicenter, first. Waves 104 feet (32 m) high crushed every house in the town, ripped the vegetation from the hills, and killed 10 people. Farther south, the island's formidable defenses barely even slowed the onslaught. After a 1983 tsunami, the town of Aonae, on the island's southern tip, had built a 15-foot-high (4.6 m) protective seawall. Now, though, swells twice that high barreled over the wall at 40 miles per hour (65 km/h). Every house facing the harbor was swept out to sea. Seven minutes later a second surge hurled fishing boats into downtown streets. From below a story of floodwater, short-circuited car horns sounded a frantic din and drowned headlights

shone on the shattered hulls of fishing boats above.

Flood and Fire

As the waters receded, flames rose. Boat batteries shorted, igniting the town's fuel supply. Blazes consumed 304 homes before fire trucks could navigate the debris-cluttered roads. Along the coast of Okushiri, the tsunami and fires demolished 437 houses and killed 198 people. In all, the earthquake and tsunami inflicted $66 million in damages upon Japan. Waves 30 feet (10 m) high also blasted the west coast of Hokkaido; they had shrunk to 13 feet (4 m) by the time they hit Russia. An hour and a half after the earthquake, the tsunami still managed to slam South Korea with 23-foot (7 m) surges.

That more people did not die was a testament to the fact that many residents knew to head for the hills when they felt the earthquake. Since 1993 Okushiri has spent 93 billion yen (over US$750 million) to protect itself from tsunamis. Every home on the island is now equipped with a special disaster radio receiver, allowing the meteorological agency to reach the public directly. The agency's operating procedure calls for alerts to be ready two minutes after an earthquake. Automatic floodgates block surges on all four major rivers, seawalls ring the coast for miles, and signs on the 40 official evacuation routes mark the heights of previous tsunamis. The south end of Aonae, obliterated in 1993, was rebuilt as a memorial park with a platform that will provide refuge for those fleeing the next monster wave.

Left: The chief engineer of the Japan Meteorological Business Support Center at work on the first day of the country's earthquake early warning system. The agency can now alert utilities, transportation companies, and hospitals as soon as it detects the first stirrings of a large earthquake.

EIGHTEENTH-CENTURY MYSTERY

In 1700 the Pacific Northwest region of the United States was uncharted territory; Europeans would not explore it for another 70 years. But it still managed to have an impact on people across the Pacific Ocean. Scientists in the late 1990s were able to link records of a January 1700 tsunami in Japan with tree-ring and geological data in North America, suggesting that a magnitude 9 earthquake along the Cascadia fault, which runs from British Columbia to California, caused the 16-foot (5 m) waves that washed over Honshu. The Japanese had not noticed an earthquake or a storm that day, and the cause of the tsunami had been a mystery for almost 300 years.

Glossary

AVALANCHE. A mass of snow, ice, soil, and rocks that flows down a hillside or mountain.

BLIZZARD. A storm in which falling snow reduces visibility to a quarter mile or less and sustained wind speeds or frequent gusts reach at least 35 miles per hour (56 km/h) for at least three hours.

CALDERA. A basin-shaped crater in a volcano, at least a mile (1.6 km) wide, formed when the eruption of magma causes the summit to collapse.

CLIMATE. The pattern of weather in an area over many years.

CLIMATOLOGIST: A scientist who studies the climate

CRUST. The brittle, outermost solid layer of the Earth; it is 3 to 5 miles thick (5 to 8 km) under the ocean and approximately 25 miles deep (40 km) below the continents.

DELTA. A triangular land area of silt and sand deposits at the mouth of a river.

EARTHQUAKE. The sudden movement of the Earth's surface caused by the release of underground stress.

EPICENTER. The point on the Earth's surface directly above where the crust began to rupture in an earthquake.

FLASH FLOOD. The sudden rise of water, usually around a stream or city.

FLOODPLAIN. A low, flat area adjacent to a river, formed by deposits of silt and subject to flooding.

FREEZING RAIN. Water droplets that fall though a shallow layer of cold air but do not freeze until they hit the ground.

GEOLOGIST. A scientist who studies the history and structure of the Earth.

GLACIAL LAKE. A body of water formed when a receding glacier carves a depression in the ground, which fills with meltwater and rain.

GLACIAL LAKE OUTBURST FLOOD. An inundation caused when a glacial lake bursts though its walls.

GLACIER. A huge field of long-lasting, slowly flowing ice formed from compacted snow.

HAIL. Lumps of frozen precipitation at least 0.2 inches (0.5 cm) in diameter that form inside thunderclouds.

HURRICANE. A tropical cyclonic storm with sustained winds of at least 74 miles per hour (119 km/h) that occurs in the North Atlantic Ocean, the Northeast Pacific Ocean east of the date line, or the South Pacific Ocean east of 160°E longitude.

LAHAR. A mudslide of volcanic debris mixed with water.

LANDSLIDE. The gravity-fueled movement of earth and debris down a slope.

LAVA. Molten rock that has reached the Earth's surface.

MAGMA. Molten rock below Earth's surface.

MAGNITUDE. The relative size or extent of an event; a measure of the energy and ground movement of an earthquake.

MANTLE. Layer of the Earth below the crust but above the core.

METEOROLOGIST. A scientist who studies the atmosphere.

MOUTH (OF A RIVER). The site where a river empties into a larger body of water.

PYROCLASTIC FLOW. An avalanche of hot volcanic gas, ash, and pieces of rock erupted by a volcano.

SEISMIC WAVE. A shock wave, generated by a earthquake, that moves through the Earth.

SEISMOLOGIST. A scientist who studies earthquakes.

SEISMOMETER. A device that records the movement of the ground.

SLEET. Frozen precipitation formed when raindrops solidify in midair into ice pellets.

SNOW. Precipitation in the form of six-sided ice crystals.

SOURCE (RIVER). The site where a river begins flowing.

TECTONIC PLATE. A block of the Earth's crust that floats on the mantle and moves in relation to the other blocks.

TORNADO. A rotating, often funnel-shaped column of air that descends from a thundercloud to contact the ground.

TROPICAL STORM. A cyclonic storm formed in the tropics whose wind speeds are between 30 and 75 miles per hour (48 to 120 km/h).

TSUNAMI. A series of large ocean waves caused by a large disturbance of the water.

VOLCANO. An opening in the Earth's surface through which molten rock and gases erupt.

VOLCANOLOGIST. A scientist who studies volcanoes.

WAVE TROUGH. The lowest point of a wave.

WETLAND. A land area that is often saturated with water.

Find Out More

BOOKS

Barry, John. *Rising Tide: The Great Mississippi Flood of 1927 and How It Changed America.* New York: Simon & Schuster, 1998.

Clark, Champ. *Flood.* Alexandria, VA: Time Life Books, 1982.

Dudley, Walter C. *Tsunami!* Honolulu: University of Hawaii Press, 1998.

Egan, Timothy. *The Worst Hard Time: The Untold Story of Those Who Survived the Great American Dust Bowl.* New York: Houghton Mifflin, 2006.

Krist, Gary. *The White Cascade: The Great Northern Railway Disaster and America's Deadliest Avalanche.* New York: Henry Holt, 2007.

Larson, Erik. *Isaac's Storm: The Drowning of Galveston, 8 September 1900.* New York: HarperCollins, 2000.

McClung, David, and Peter Schaerer. *The Avalanche Handbook.* Seattle: Mountaineers Books, 1993.

McCullough, David G. *Johnstown Flood.* New York: Simon & Schuster, 1968.

Tremper, Bruce. *Staying Alive in Avalanche Terrain.* Seattle: Mountaineers Books, 2001.

Winchester, Simon. *Krakatoa: The Day the World Exploded, August 27th, 1883.* New York: HarperCollins, 2003.

WEB SITES

Canadian Broadcasting Corporation archives of the 1998 ice storm, http://archives.cbc.ca/IDD-1-70-258/disasters_tragedies/ice_storm/

Johnstown (PA) Area Heritage Association's history of the Johnstown flood, www.jaha.org/FloodMuseum/history.html

Museum of the City of San Francisco's earthquake archives, www.sfmuseum.org

National Climatic Data Center, the world's largest archive of climate data, www.ncdc.noaa.gov

National Oceanic & Atmospheric Administration, www.noaa.gov

National Weather Service, www.weather.gov

National Weather Service hurricane page, www.weather.gov/os/hurricane/index.shtml

NOAA drought information center, www.drought.noaa.gov

NOAA El Niño page, www.elnino.noaa.gov

NOAA hurricane page, http://hurricanes.noaa.gov

NOAA tornado portal, www.noaa.gov/tornadoes.html

Pacific Tsunami Museum, www.tsunami.org/index.html

PBS American Experience: The Dust Bowl, www.pbs.org/wgbh/amex/dustbowl

PBS American Experience: The 1927 Mississippi Flood, www.pbs.org/wgbh/amex/flood/index.html

PBS, Nova tracks El Niño, www.pbs.org/wgbh/nova/elnino

U.S. Geological Survey home page, www.usgs.gov

U.S. Geological Survey data on world volcanoes, www.usgs.gov/hazards/volcanoes

Volcano World, sponsored by the NASA North Dakota Space Grant Consortium, http://volcano.und.edu

At the Smithsonian

National Museum of Natural History, Global Volcanism Program

For nearly 40 years, the Global Volcanism Program (GVP) has worked toward a clearer understanding of the planet's active volcanoes. The GVP, as part of the Department of Mineral Sciences in the National Museum of Natural History, maintains a database cataloging each volcano that has erupted in the past 10,000 years. The program also serves as a clearinghouse for information during the often confusing early stages of current eruptions. The GVP publishes a monthly bulletin with reports on up to 25 volcanoes. You can find out more about the program on its Web site: www.volcano.si.edu.

Lava flow in Hawaii Volcanoes National Park. Volcanic activity is monitored by Smithsonian's Global Volcanism Program (GVP), which maintains an extensive database.

National Air and Space Museum, Center for Earth and Planetary Studies

Using data from satellites and space missions, the Center for Earth and Planetary Studies (CEPS) researches a number of geological processes, including volcanism, flooding, and tectonics, on Earth and other planets. CEPS (www.nasm.si.edu/ceps) also maintains an archive of many of NASA's planetary images, including an extensive collection taken from the Space Shuttle. CEPS employees curate, among other exhibits, the Looking at Earth Gallery in the National Air and Space Museum, which illustrates how aerial photography has improved our understanding of the world we live in.

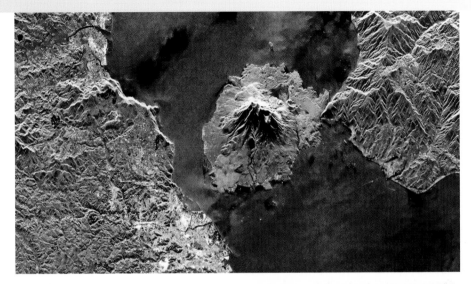

Left: This radar image taken from the Space Shuttle shows the active Sakurajima volcano on Kyushu Island, Japan. The Smithsonian's Center for Earth and Planetary Studies maintains an archive of images that include many taken from the Space Shuttle.

Below: Exterior view of the National Air and Space Museum. This popular Smithsonian museum includes the Center for Earth and Planetary Studies (CEPS), where research on many geological processes is conducted.

National Zoological Park, Conservation and Research Center

The mission of the CRC (http://nationalzoo.si.edu/conservationandscience) is "the conservation of biodiversity through scientific research, professional training, and environmental education." The CRC is one of the most extensive conservation biology research programs in the world, employing scientists in ecology and biodiversity monitoring, reproduction and animal health, genetic diversity, and nutrition and geographic information systems. The scientists seek to conserve existing wildlife and return endangered species to their natural habitats. The CRC also trains government officials, wildlife managers, teachers, and students from around in the world in conservation.

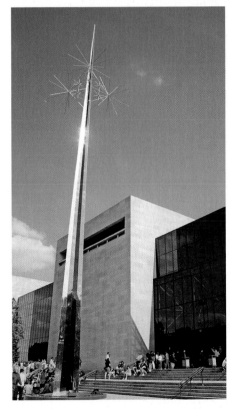

National Museum of Natural History

Dedicated to "inspiring curiosity, discovery, and learning about the natural world through its unparalleled research, collections, exhibitions, and education outreach programs," the Museum of Natural History, which will celebrate a century on the national mall in Washington, D.C., in 2010, houses exhibits and sponsors research on topics from the cultures of Africa to the beauty of rare gemstones. The collection houses more than 126 million specimens and cultural artifacts, including dinosaur bones, Moon rocks, and the Hope diamond. The Museum's research activities are organized into seven departments— anthropology, botany, entomology, invertebrate zoology, mineral sciences, paleobiology, and vertebrate zoology. Find out more on their Web site: www.mnh.si.edu.

Exterior view of the National Museum of Natural History. Housing a wide array of collections and exhibitions, the museum is one of the largest and most comprehensive research facilities in the world.

Hurricane Digital Memory Bank

The Smithsonian's National Museum of American History is one of 20 partners in the Hurricane Digital Memory Bank, an electronic archive of information on Hurricanes Katrina and Rita (2005). Project workers maintain the record of these storms, collecting information from various sources, including firsthand accounts of survivors and on-scene images. The information is kept available online for researchers (http://hurricanearchive.org/browse/?collection=10).

Above: Aerial photograph of Hurricane Gordon, September 17, 2006.

Left: Joseph Henry, the first director of the Smithsonian Institution, was a pioneer in the development of modern weather reporting technology.

Smithsonian Institution Archives, Joseph Henry Papers Project

Joseph Henry was the first director of the Smithsonian Institution in 1846. He also organized a series of weather reporting stations that were connected by telegraph, which became the U.S. Weather Bureau (later the National Weather Service) in 1891. The Joseph Henry Papers Project (http://siarchives.si.edu) is a collection of 110,000 of the scientist's documents, the most important of which were published in *The Papers of Joseph Henry* (Smithsonian Institution Press). The project workers also maintain a searchable digital index. Henry's work led to advances in telegraphy, telephony, aeronautics, and the electric motor.

Index

Acknowledgments and Credits

The author thanks Jennifer Hoffman of the University of Washington for her work as consultant on this book. The author would also like to thank Ben Oderwald and Richard Snow, Fred Allen, and the rest of the staff of *American Heritage* magazine.

The author and publisher offer thanks to those closely involved in the creation of this volume: Andrew Johnston, National Air and Space Museum, Smithsonian Institution; Ellen Nanney, Senior Brand Manager, Katie Mann, and Carolyn Gleason with Smithsonian Business Ventures; Collins Reference executive editor Donna Sanzone, editor Lisa Hacken, and editorial assistant Stephanie Meyers; Hydra Publishing president Sean Moore, publishing director Karen Prince, senior editor Molly Morrison, art director Brian MacMullen, designers Ken Crossland, Erika Lubowicki, and Lisa Purcell, production editors Eunho Lee and Lee Bartow, editorial director Aaron Murray, picture researcher Ben DeWalt, editors Rachael Lanicci, Suzanne Lander, Andy Lawler, Gabrielle Kappes, and Michael Smith; copy editor Glenn Novak; indexer Jessie Shiers; and Akiko Harayama of ReliefWeb/United Nations.

Credits

The following abbreviations are used: AP—Associated Press; ERL—Environmental Research Laboratory; FEMA—Federal Emergency Management Agency; GSFC—Goddard Space Flight Center; IO—Index Open; JI—© 2007 Jupiterimages Corporatin; LoC—Library of Congress; NASA—National Aeronautics and Space Administration; NGDC—National Geophysical Data Center; NOAA—National Oceanic & Atmospheric Administration; NOS—National Ocean Service; NSSL—National Severe Storms Laboratory; NWS—National Weather Service; OAR—Oceanic and Atmospheric Research; ORR—Office of Response and Restoration (NOAA); PR—Photo Researchers, Inc.; SPL—Science Photo Library; SS—ShutterStock; SXG—stock.xchng; USGS—US Geological Survey

Earth's Destructive Power
iv-vbg NOAA iv NOAA v NOAA vi Krafft 1 FEMA/Andrea Booher 2 USGS 3tr FEMA/Mark Wolfe 3b FEMA/Robert A. Eplett 4—5bg Hylas Publishing 6bg SS/Frank Anusewicz 6bg SS/Lisa F. Young 7bg SS/James R. Hearn 8—9bg USGS 10—11bg AP

Chapter 1: Hurricanes
12—13bg Wikimedia 14tl AP 14bg NASA/Jeff Schmaltz 16 Hylas Publishing. Data source: University of Illinois at Urbana-Champaign 17t NASA-GSFC 17r NOAA 18 SS/Tad Denson 19 NASA-GSFC 20 Marvin Nauman/FEMA 21 Bob McMillan/FEMA 22 NASA and Digital Globe 24 Hylas Publishing. Data source: NASA 25 NASA 26 NASA-GSFC and ORBIMAGE 27 Dave Saville/FEMA 28 Liz Roll/FEMA 29 NASA-GSFC 30 Hylas Publishing. Data Source: USGS 31 Debbie Larson, Historic NWS Collection/NOAA 32 Debbie Larson, Historic NWS Collection/NOAA 33 AP/Scott Dalton 34 NOAA Historic NWS Collection 35 LoC 36 AP 37tr LoC 37bc LoC

Chapter 2: Tornadoes
38tl Win Henderson/FEMA 38bg NGIC/Carsten Peter 40bl Hylas Publishing 40tr NOAA/OAR/ERL/NSSL 42 AP/Pavel Rhaman 43 AP/Pavel Rhaman 44 NOAA/Historic NWS Collection 45tl NOAA/Historic NWS Collection 45tr NOAA/Historic NWS Collection 46 AP 47 PR/Joseph Golden 48 NOAA/OAR/ERL/NSSL 49 Andrea Booher/FEMA 50 NOAA/OAR/ERL/NSSL 51 Andrea Booher/FEMA 52 NOAA/Paul Huffman 53 AP/Elam Smith 54 Hylas Publishing 55bl PR/Jim Reed 55tr NOAA/OAR/ERL/NSSL 56bl PR/Reed Timmer and Jim Bishop/Jim Reed Photography 56tr NASA 57 Linda Winkler/FEMA

Chapter 3: Ice Storms, Snowstorms, and Avalanches
58tl PR/M. Kulyk 58bg SS/Aleksander Bolbot 60—61bg SS/Joy Fera 60 IO/photolibrary.com 61 NOAA/Historic NWS Collection 62 Hylas Publishing. Data source: Wikimedia/Norman Einstein. 63 Wikimedia/Jan Zatko 64 AP/Dick Blume 65tr AP/Jaques Boissinot 65bl Wikimedia/Robert Lawton 66 NASA 67 IO/Keith Levit Photography 68 NOAA/Historic NWS Collection/Elizabeth A. Hobbs 69t AP/Ron Frehm 70—71bg Jim Reed/SPL 70 SS/Mircea Bezergheanu 71 AP/Dieter Endlicher 72bg NASA 72 NASA/Jaques Descloitres 73tr Hylas Publishing. Data source: maps-of-china.com 73br NOAA/OAR/ERL/NSSL 74 SXG/mffavilez 75 USGS 76 USGS 77 USGS 78—79bg SS/byphoto 78 LoC/Picket Photo Co. 79tr LoC 79br Andrea Booher/FEMA

Chapter 4: Floods and Their Consequences
80tl AP/Pavel Rahman 80bg NASA-GSFC 82tl SS/Bartlomiej K. Kwieciszewski 82br ? 83 JI 85 NASA 86 AP/Pavel Rahman 87 AP/Pavel Rahman 88 Hylas Publishing. Data source: Wikimedia 89 NOAA/NOS/ORR/Dr. Terry McTigue 90 LoC 91tr NOAA/Historic NWS Collection/Steve Nicklas 91br AP/James A. Finley 92 NOAA/Historic NWS Collection/Steve Nicklas 93t LoC/DeSouza Bros./Harris & Ewing 93cl LoC/Felix J. Koch 93br SS/Sharon Meredith 95 SS/TAOLMOR 95inset Wikimedia 96bg. Wikimedia 97 AP/Wang Song 98 LoC 99 NOAA/Historic NWS Collection/Steve Nicklas 100 NOAA/Historic NWS Collection/Steve Nicklas 101 AP 102—103bg Wikimedia/Raymond Ostertag 103t AP/Brennan Linsley 103b AP/Mario Cruz 104 NASA Jet Propulsion Labortory/Bill Ofenheim 105 AP/Scott Dalton

Chapter 5: Drought and Heat Waves
106tl NASA Earth Observatory 106bg SS/Suzanne Long 108tr JI 108c JI 108—109bg Gary James Calder 109tr Wikimedia/Demosh 109br SS/Jim Parkin 110—111bg NOAA/George E. Marsh Album 112 Historic NWS Collection 113 Historic NWS Collection 115 AP 116bg NASA Earth Observatory/Jesse Allen 117 AP/Wang Chengxuan 117bg SS/Louise Shumbris 118bg NASA Visible Earth 119 SS/Socrates 120—21 NASA 121 JI 123 AP/Siddharth Darshan Kumar 123 AP/Siddharth Darshan Kumar 124 NASA Earth Observatory/Retro Stockli and Robert Simmons 125 AP/Frank Prevel 126bg SS/Ximaglination 126 AP/Geoff Spencer 127 SS/Chris Burt 128 SS/Sascha Burkard 129 NASA Earth Observatory/Jacques Descloitres 130bl NASA-GSFC 130br NASA 131 SS/Galyana Andrushko

Chapter 6: Earthquakes
132—33 USGS/James G. Moore 134tl SPL/Simon Fraser 134bg USGS 136 NASA 137bg SPL/David Parker 137tr SPL/Russel D. Curtis 138 NASA 139 US Navy/Timothy Smith 140 Hylas Publishing. Data source: LoC 141 NASA/Earth Observatory 140—41bg SS/Vladimir Melnik 142 NOAA-NGDC 143 AP/Eric Marti 144 Christian Von Wissel/Wiki 145 USGS 146 USGS 147 USGS 148 Wikimedia 149 USGS 150—51bg US Dept of Defense 151 LoC 152 USGS/R.M. Hamilton 153 LoC 154 USGS 155tl USGS 155br USGS

Chapter 7: Volcanoes
156tl IO/Keith Levit Photography 156bg USGS 158 Wikimedia/Giorgio Sommer 159tr PR/Mikkel Juul Jensen 159bc Hylas Publishing. Data source: Wikimedia 161 PR/David Weintraub 162 PR/NASA 163 PR/Gordon Gerradd 164 PR/Jeremy Bishop 165t SS/Stuart Taylor 165br PR/David Hardy 166 SS/Albert Barr 167tl LoC 167br USGS 168tl LoC 168br LoC 169 LoC 170 PR/Bernhard Edmaier 171tl PR/Stephen & Donna O'Meara 171br PR/Stephen & Donna O'Meara 172 USGS 174 USGS 175bg 175 USGS/Washington State DOT 176 SS/Bryan Busoviki 177l USGS 177r SS/Brian Schlittenhardt 178 PR/Hoa-Qui 179 PR/Philippe Bourseiller 180 NASA/Planetary Photojournal 181 Hylas Publishing. Data source: USGS 182 Wikimedia 183 AP

Chapter 8: Tsunamis
184tl SS/Pavel Kapish 184bg USGS 186 USGS 187 SS/Sebastian Kaulitzki 188 SS/Steven Collins 189 Created by the ReliefWeb Map Centre, United Nations Office for the coordination of Humanitarian Affairs 190 SS/A.S. Zain 191 Wikimedia 192tr SS/salamanderman 192bl SS/Steven Collins 193l NASA 193r NASA 194 SS/Yanik Chauvin 195l NGDC/US Coast Guard 195r NGDC/US Coast Guard 196 NGDC 197t Pierre St. Amand 197b Pacific Tide Party 198tr SS/Vera Bogaerts 198b NGDC 199 NGDC 200 Wikimedia 201 NASA 202tl Hylas Publishing. Data source: NOAA 202bl AP/Katsumi Kasahara 203 AP/Katsumi Kasahara

At the Smithsonian
208 SS/Bryan Busovicki 209 SI/Laurie Minor-Penland 209 SI 210 SI/James Di Laureto 211inset NASA 211t NOAA Archives

Cover Art
Front PR/David Weintraub Back Wikimedia

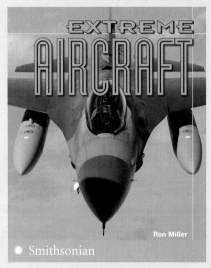
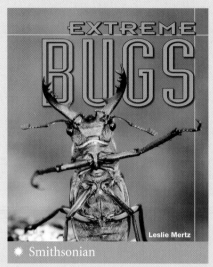
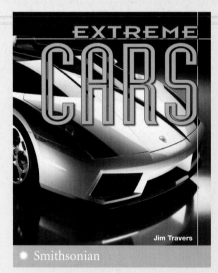
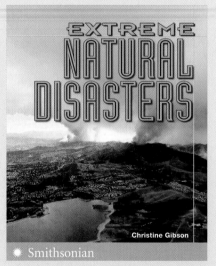

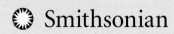